How to Buy and Restore Wicker Furniture

by
Thomas Duncan

DUNCAN-HOLMES PUBLISHING COMPANY
SYRACUSE, INDIANA

Library of Congress Catalog Card Number 82-73902
International Standard Book Number:
  0-9609480-0-7   (hardbound)
  0-9609480-1-5   (paperbound)

First edition published July, 1983
2nd printing ... September, 1983

Duncan-Holmes Publishing Company
P.O. Box 481
Syracuse, Indiana 46567

ACKNOWLEDGEMENTS

The making of this book has not been a solitary task. I wish to thank James Wortham for his unselfish devotion of time and publishing expertise, and Richard Holmes whose enthusiasm and generosity have made this book a reality.

Also, I am grateful to Jeanne and Colby Holmes for their assistance with the photographs, Sandra Buhrt for her darkroom work, and Virginia Xanders for her editorial assistance.

For Sylvia, whose untiring work and writing contributions have been invaluable in creating this book.

CONTENTS

INTRODUCTION   1

I   WHAT IS WICKER?   2

II   BUYING RESTORABLE WICKER   3
       Why buy and restore old wicker?   3
       Five minute checklist   4
       Where to go to buy wicker   14

III PREPARATION   17
       Introduction to repair   17
       Tools and materials   19
       Using reed, cane, and fiber rush   21

IV   REPAIRS   25

V   FINISHING   146

     APPENDICES   159
       A. Suppliers   159
       B. General working tips   160

     GLOSSARY   161

     BIBLIOGRAPHY   162

     INDEX   163

INTRODUCTION

Wicker furniture and accessories are making a comeback. Many people are rediscovering wicker's versatility, lightness, tastefulness, and comfort as they place it not only in the traditional role on the porch but also in the living room, bedroom, and bath. Wicker is appropriate in today's settings ranging from country homes to city apartments and performs both its old and new roles with beauty and style.

Wicker produced in America between the mid-1800's to the 1930's is being actively sought by collectors, decorators, and many others who wish to add its elegance and comfort to their own homes. Sometimes old wicker can be found in mint condition, but often, since over the years many pieces were subjected to weather and given hard use, there are varying amounts of damage to the woven material and, perhaps, even to the framework. My purpose in writing this book is to prove this damage can be <u>inexpensively</u> and <u>easily</u> repaired, and older wicker can be completely restored to its original function and beauty by <u>you</u> in your own home!

I have been professionally engaged in wicker repair and painting for seven years. This book is based upon my experience in a wide variety of challenging repair situations. This is not an historical perspective of the wicker furniture industry nor is it a dollars and cents guide for the collector; these areas are already sufficiently explored in the current literature (see Bibliography, p. 162). My purpose is to present you with a tried and true system for evaluating the condition of the wicker you see in the marketplace and then to provide step-by-step restoration techniques accompanied by detailed photographs so you can go about making the necessary repairs with skill and confidence.

Wicker repair provides an enjoyable challenge with endless variety. Every piece requires a different approach, and very dramatic effects can be achieved with simple yet sound repairs. Many times I have received a heavily damaged chair and transformed it into a sound, whole chair with a sparkling finish. Often the delighted owner's response is, "This is <u>mine</u>? I didn't recognize it. I'll have to find a place for this where it <u>shows</u>!"

I. WHAT IS WICKER?

Wicker is not a material, but a generic term referring to furniture woven from any of a number of materials such as rattan, willow, reed, and raffia, to name a few. Pliant twigs from other types of plants are also used, but this book will only concern itself with furniture made from reed and cane obtained from the rattan palm and manmade fiber rush. These materials are readily obtained, easily worked, and are used in the vast majority of pieces on the market today.

Some of the most commonly used materials for making wicker furniture are obtained from the rattan palm which is indigenous to the East Indies. The rattan palm is actually a vine which grows to several hundred feet in length. The bark of rattan is removed and cut into strips used in making cane seats and backs for chairs, and in wrapping various parts of furniture framework. After the bark has been removed from the rattan vine and made into cane, the remaining part is either used to make the legs and framework of rattan furniture or is machine cut into reed of various diameters and shapes, for example, round reed, flat reed, and half round reed. Reed made from the rattan palm was first used in making furniture in the mid-19th century and is still used today.

Until 1904 all wicker furniture was made with natural materials, but in this year manmade fiber rush was invented. Fiber rush is produced by twisting paper; it is strong, pliable, and inexpensive. A revolution in wicker furniture came in 1917 when Marshall Lloyd invented a machine to weave sheets of fiber rush. After these large sheets were woven on Lloyd's loom they were draped and fitted over the frameworks. Thus, Lloyd was able to eliminate much of the laborious handweaving involved in producing wicker from reed and to use less expensive materials for the weaving. Along with this low cost came the inevitable loss of intricate detail that could only be produced by a skilled craftsman. From a utilitarian point of view, however, it makes no difference whether a piece of furniture is made from reed or fiber rush; one is as desirable as the other provided it is in good condition.

II. BUYING RESTORABLE WICKER

Why Buy and Restore Old Wicker?

Suppose you are remodeling your home and plan to enclose the screened-in porch so it may be used the year around. You want to keep the room light and airy. Buy and restore wicker!

You may be a young married couple furnishing a first apartment. You need a few comfortable pieces of furniture: something you can enjoy now and yet will be suitable later when you have your own home. Good quality new furniture is cumbersome to move and so very expensive. Buy and restore wicker!

Perhaps you have just purchased a turn of the century home and want to decorate in keeping with its history. Buy and restore wicker!

You have inherited your grandmother's ornate Victorian rocker. Everyone says it's beautiful but it needs a little repair work. You can do the work yourself. Pieces you have restored as an enjoyable hobby in your free time may be added to your collection or sold at a good profit.

Beauty, comfort, period decor, an enjoyable pastime, and even profit are all sound reasons for buying and restoring wicker. When you purchase and restore a piece of early American-made wicker you possess a valuable century-old antique. Even though much old wicker in the market has not reached its hundredth birthday, and therefore does not technically qualify as a true antique, wicker made as late as the 1930's is considered highly desirable and collectible. The quality of materials and workmanship far exceeds that of today's modern reproductions.

All the persons mentioned in the foregoing examples will enter the marketplace with different ideas of what they are looking for in wicker furniture. Before setting out to buy, ask yourself these questions:

- Where am I going to put the wicker?
- Will the furniture get daily, seasonal, or decorative use?
- What will be its purpose in my decorating scheme?

THE FIVE MINUTE CHECKLIST

In the years I have been doing restoration I have taken hundreds of wicker pieces useless in their damaged conditions and have transformed them into beautiful, functional furniture. Occasionally, however, I receive an excited phone call from a beginning collector who tells me about a wonderful bargain they picked up at a sale or flea market. Unfortunately, when the enthusiastic client brings the piece to me for repair, a quick inspection will tell me the piece needs very extensive repair or is irreparable. Their bargain is sometimes relegated to my bin of spare parts.

This chapter will show you how to avoid a bad purchase by detailing a simple, five minute checklist for the evaluation of the present condition of a piece and determination of the extent and feasibility of repairs. If a piece rates highly on the list you can be confident of the purchase. If, on the other hand, the adorable-but-too-brittle-to-ever-be-sat-upon-again Victorian rocker can be had at a bargain price it will be understood that, at best, it may only be suitable for holding a china doll on display in the guest room. Romantic visions of rocking away your retirement years upon it are gently, but thoroughly, dispelled.

The checklist may be used by buyers on all levels of expertise. The novice collector can use it to estimate what skills and materials are needed to do the restoration work. An antique dealer who hires a professional for restoration can make good use of the checklist to determine the top dollar to bid in order to pay for all the repairs and still make a profit on the resale market.

Refer to the checklist when shopping. After using the list several times, your practiced eye will automatically give each piece a thorough "run down." You will find it is a simple matter to become a knowledgeable collector of beautiful, functional wicker furniture and accessories.

How the Checklist Works

To evaluate a piece of wicker you must consider three physical attributes: (1) the condition of the woven material, (2) the basic quality and soundness of the framework underlying the woven material, and (3) the condition of the finish, whether painted or natural. These three categories form the basis of the checklist.

Under each category are conditions to look for listed in order of difficulty of repair. The simplest to repair is at the top and the level of challenge increases as you read down the column. Beside each condition is a page number which refers you to the restoration technique to be used to correct the damage. These page numbers are not intended to be used while performing the five minute check. They will serve later as a guide for locating the specific repair techniques.

The conditions have been loosely divided into four skill levels: (I) Easy to master—Quick to do, (II) Moderately easy—More time consuming, (III) More difficult to master—Repairs of complex nature, and (IV) Irreparable—Piece cannot be restored to former function and/or beauty.

I am not able to list in detail all the specific conditions you may find when wicker hunting. This checklist contains the most common restoration problems I see every day in my business and ones which I show you how to solve in this book.

The labeled chairs below are an aid for using the checklist. The terminology detailed here will also help you when beginning your repairs.

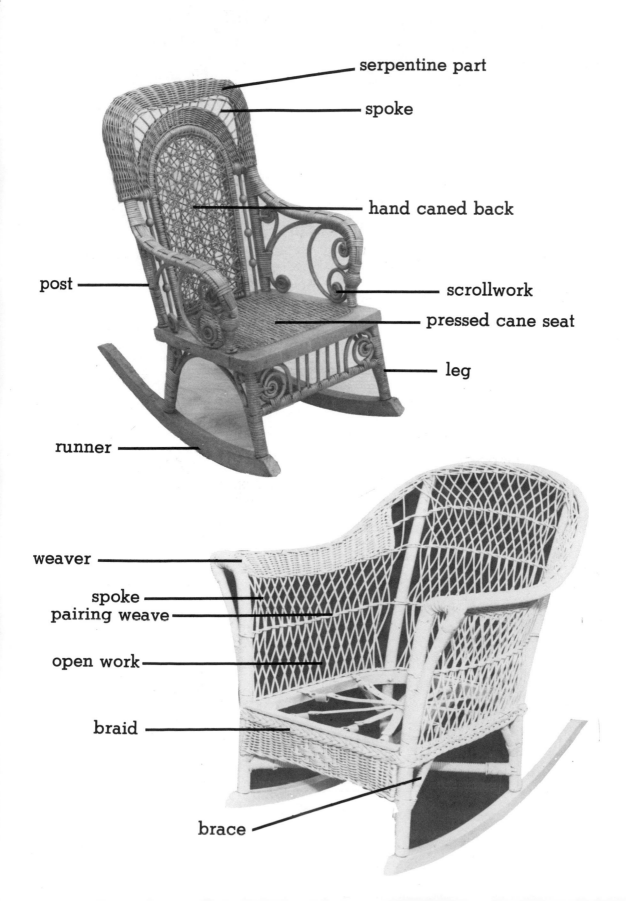

serpentine part

spoke

hand caned back

post

scrollwork

pressed cane seat

leg

runner

weaver

spoke

pairing weave

open work

braid

brace

FIVE MINUTE CHECKLIST

SKILL LEVELS	WOVEN MATERIAL	FRAMEWORK	FINISH
EASY TO MASTER— QUICK TO DO I	SAGGING CANE SEAT 160 WRAPPING MISSING 44-47 WEAVERS BROKEN/MISSING IN SPOTS 24-27 SPOKES BROKEN/MISSING IN SPOTS 32-43, LOOSE SCROLLWORK 94-95 BROKEN PAIRING WEAVE 28-29 BRAID DAMAGED IN SPOTS 48-51 BROKEN/MISSING WEAVERS ON SERPENTINE ARM 104-107	BRACES ON FRAME LOOSE 59 LOOSE RUNNERS 82-85	DIRTY 147 NEEDS TOUCH UP TO EITHER PAINTED OR NATURAL FINISH 152-153 PAINTED LEG CAPS 156-157
MODERATELY EASY— MORE TIME CONSUMING II	HEAVILY DAMAGED OR MISSING BRAID 52-57 BROKEN/MISSING CANE SEAT 138-145 MISSING SKIRT 124-131 BROKEN SPOKES ON SERPENTINE PARTS 108-109 MISSING SCROLLWORK 96-101 HOLE IN WOVEN MATERIAL 30-31	BROKEN SLAT UNDER SEAT 66-67 JOINTS ON FRAME LOOSE 60-63 BROKEN OR MISSING SPRINGS 74-81 BROKEN DOWEL UNDER SEAT 64-67 BROKEN TENON ON LEG GOING INTO RUNNER 86-87 FLOOR LAMP OR STAND LEANS 132-136	NEEDS ALL OVER PAINT OR VARNISH JOB 153, 154, 155
MORE DIFFICULT TO MASTER— REPAIRS OF COMPLEX NATURE III	EXTENSIVE DAMAGE TO SPOKES AND WEAVERS ON SERPENTINE AREAS 110-117	SPLIT/PEELING TABLE TOP 118-123 MISSING/DAMAGED RUNNERS ON CHAIR 88-93 BROKEN POST/LEG 68-73	CRACKED/CHIPPED PAINT 12-13, 147, 148 HAS BEEN STRIPPED— FUZZY AND BRITTLE 147, 148, 149-151
IRREPARABLE— PIECE CANNOT BE RESTORED TO FORMER FUNCTION AND/OR BEAUTY IV	NO WIRE IN BROKEN SPOKES ACROSS BACK FIBER COUCH OR CHAIR BRITTLE FIBER RUSH/ REED; SNAPS IMMEDIATELY WHEN BENT (LIKE SPAGHETTI)	UNCOMFORTABLE FRAMEWORK ROTTEN	GLOBBY PAINT FILLING ALL HOLES IN WEAVE BADLY WEATHERED FIBER RUSH

1

2

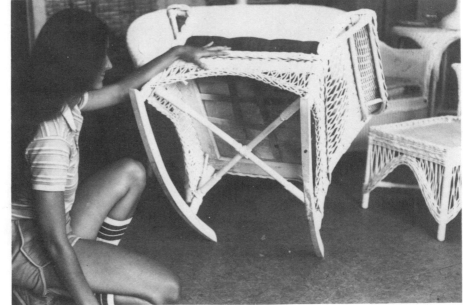

Follow this wicker buyer as she goes through the process of evaluating several items for her home.

Photo 1

First, sit in the chair. Check for comfort. Does the contour of the chair back fit your back? Is the chair back free of bumpy, uncomfortable braid or support bars? If a rocker, is the backward angle correct or does the chair lean back too far? Shift your weight around and gently wiggle the arms. Does the chair feel solid?

Photo 2

Turn the chair over to inspect the framework. Check carefully for any broken, loose, or missing parts.

While you are looking underneath, you will want to determine whether the piece is constructed of fiber rush or reed. Inspect the loose ends. Look for telltale diagonal grooves and ragged ends that differentiate the twisted paper of fiber rush from natural reed.

3

4

Photo 3

If you find a piece of wicker with extensive damage to the woven work, especially in many separate areas, inspect with particular attention to the suppleness of the reed or fiber rush. If the woven material is very brittle (snaps like spaghetti when bent), it is not worth repairing if it is a piece that is weight bearing, such as a chair or couch.

Photo 4

Our wicker buyer also uncovered this broken chair in a back room. The only flaw in the fiber rush chair is that the spokes are broken close to the top. This would appear to be a relatively easy thing to correct; however, this chair was poorly constructed using weight-bearing spokes without wire cores and cannot hold up to the stress.) *and will break.* These spokes could be replaced in their entirety (see Replacing Spokes in Entirety, p. 42) to make a sound repair, but it is very difficult to replace spokes in a tightly woven (loom woven) piece of this type since the spokes must be forced into place through many tight rows of weavers. Even if you could fix the broken spokes, the remaining spokes are still of inferior construction and will break.

5

6

Photo 5

This loveseat could be deceiving. At first glance, the woven work looks intact and it doesn't appear to need any repair—just a good cleaning, sanding and a new paint job.

Photo 6

However, look at the woven material up close. The finish is in terrible condition. Paint that isn't cracked or flaking has been very thickly applied over this fiber rush material. Since stripping is impossible (see "The Pros and Cons of Stripping," p. 149-151), the surface is very uneven and unattractive. Sanding will help to smooth the roughest areas of paint, but will roughen the exposed paper. Also, it must be understood that even with a carefully applied primer and top coat, this loveseat can never regain a smooth, attractive finish. The owners probably subjected this piece to the extremes of weather and even though the woven material is intact, our smart wicker buyer will pass by this "bargain."

Now that she has inspected the framework, woven material, and finish, she tallies the things that need correction, keeping in mind the levels of difficulty of the needed repairs. If most repairs are in skill levels I and II, they should be relatively simple to perform. If in II and III, she will need to spend more time and perhaps have more tools at hand to complete the repairs. If in level IV, in most instances, the piece cannot be used for its original purpose. If the piece is still irresistible, our buyer will keep her offer low.

Her bargaining power increases as she demonstrates to a dealer that she knows what to look for when she shops. She may find repairable flaws of which even the dealer is unaware and perhaps can negotiate the price to her advantage. This is how taking the checklist along is like going shopping with an expert in restoration.

Where to Go to Buy Wicker

Grab this book and let's go buy some wicker! Now that you are prepared to evaluate realistically what you see, you will discover that wicker crops up everywhere for sale and finding bargains is fun. A beginning collector need only watch public sale notices or attend area flea markets to find an opportunity to purchase restorable wicker. Household auctions will sometimes provide a chance to bid on matching pieces while flea markets and yard sales may offer unique, one-of-a-kind items to the person willing to do some treasure hunting.

Don't forget to visit your area antique shops. Perhaps the piece or pieces you want will be on display, restored or not, at a price you can well afford. Some further snooping may yield a beautiful item in desperate need of restoration that can be had at a very good price since you can do the repairs yourself. Frequenting antique shops can also give you an education in styles of wicker furniture and current market values.

Also take some time to look at the current line of new reproduction wicker furniture in your area furniture stores. Carefully compare the quality of craftsmanship and materials. Note the prices you encounter. This bit of research will convince you that, for lasting value, a carefully restored and finished older piece will give you a lifetime of service far surpassing the usefulness of new wicker on the market.

III. PREPARATION

Introduction to Repair

These general methods will stand one in good stead regardless of what type or style of wicker furniture is to be repaired. The general principles in Chapters III and IV are based on sound repair methods—the key to quality restoration of any type of wicker furniture.

After you understand the general repair methods, the only other information you need for perfect restoration is right before your eyes. Study the piece you are restoring. Simply apply these principles and your own powers of observation in order to duplicate the pattern of the existing design. In the majority of cases, my photographs will show you exactly how to restore the piece you are repairing, but since there are so many different pieces of wicker furniture, many with their own individuality, no book can cover how to restore each one. You will soon discover that good wicker restoration is exciting detective work.

Let your personality and the quality of the piece dictate the degree of craftsmanship needed. You may desire only a sound, usable repair or you may decide to do as I do and restore your beautiful wicker so the repairs are completely undetectable.

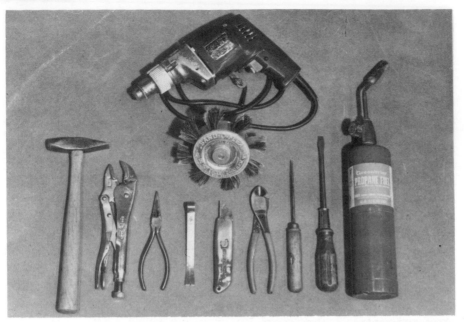

1

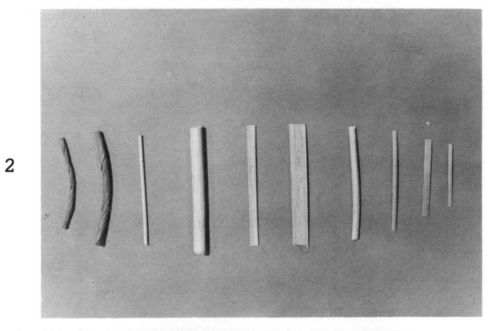

2

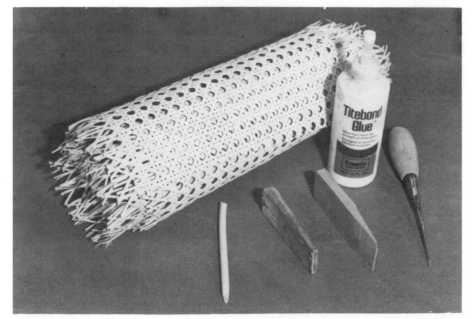

3

Tools and Materials

Photo 1

Most wicker can be restored with the few simple tools pictured. Included are a hammer, VISE-GRIP® pliers, needle nose pliers, tack lifter, utility knife, diagonal cutters, ice pick, screwdriver, propane torch, Sand-O-Flex® sander and an electric drill. A word of caution concerning the seemingly innocuous needle nose pliers: if the plier tips should slip off a piece of reed or fiber rush that is being forcibly pushed or pulled through the weave, there exists the possibility of being struck on the other hand or even in the face by the sharp points. Please guard against this danger by safely positioning your hands, face, and tool.

For a person such as myself, who handles a large volume of furniture. I find an air compressor, spray gun and air powered stapler invaluable. I recommend the purchase of the Senco J series staple gun which has saved me countless hours thus making my repairs more profitable and enjoyable. See Appendix A, p. 159, for the address of Merit Abrasive Products and Senco Fastening Systems.

Photo 2

Some of the more commonly used materials for repairing wicker are, left to right, two sizes of fiber rush, two sizes of round reed, two sizes of flat reed, two sizes of half-round reed, and two sizes of cane. A much larger variety of sizes is available through the suppliers listed in Appendix A on page 159.

Photo 3

These are the tools and materials needed to install a pressed cane seat: pressed cane, spline, wide and narrow ended wedges, Titebond® glue (see Appendix A, p. 159), and a narrow chisel.

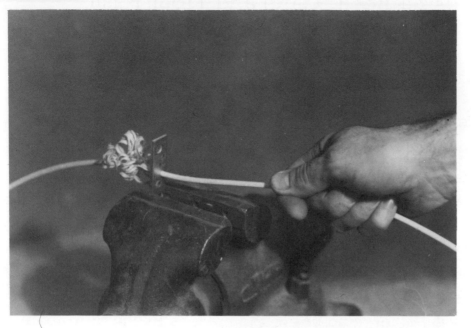

1

2

Using Reed, Cane and Fiber Rush

REDUCING DIAMETER OF ROUND REED

Photo 1

There are two basic reasons for reducing the diameter of round reed: either the correct size is not obtainable or only a small amount of round reed of a certain diameter is needed and the reed on hand is too large. To reduce the diameter of round reed, drill a hole in a piece of steel (of the diameter desired), clamp the steel in a vise, whittle the end of the reed to size, insert the end through the hole in the steel and merely pull it through. A pair of VISE-GRIPS® is handy for starting the first few inches.

The reed must be dry. Wet reed compresses instead of being shaved down in diameter when pulled through the hole. Often, the reed needs to be pulled through at least twice to be reduced smoothly. A light sanding with fine sandpaper will remove any roughness on the reed. If the reed is being reduced a considerable amount in diameter the process may require an intermediate reduction before final sizing.

Photo 2

This is an example of a piece of steel used for reducing the diameter of round reed. It is approximately 6" long by 1" wide and 1/8" thick. The metal should be of a shape that is easily secured in a vise and can be readily drilled.

REED AND CANE

All reed and cane should be soaked in warm water before using to make repairs. This increases the suppleness of the material. Cane and the smaller diameters of reed need only be soaked for a few minutes. Larger diameter reed may need to be soaked up to fifteen minutes. When making scrollwork from large diameter reed, it is sometimes necessary to soak the reed in very hot water to facilitate the making of extreme bends. Reed should not be soaked for excessive periods of time lest small fibers or whiskerlike projections be raised on the surface.

FIBER RUSH

Do not soak fiber rush. It is ready to use as is.

USE OF GLUE ON WOVEN MATERIAL

Very few repairs to the woven material require the use of glue. In a properly executed repair, the woven material holds itself in place better than glue ever could. Unless specifically mentioned, the use of glue is unnecessary.

1

2

3

IV. REPAIRS

Repairing Broken Weavers by Piecing

One often finds numerous small spots on wicker where the weavers are broken or missing. These spots are easily fixed by piecing with a small length of weaver. For additional information on replacing weavers, refer to "Piecing Weavers On Serpentine Arm."

Photo 1

This lamp shade has a broken weaver.

Photo 2

Cut off the damaged weaver on the inside of the lamp shade. The weaver is cut directly over the spoke. This leaves the exposed end hidden while it is still held securely in place.

Photo 3

Insert a new weaver from the outside.

4

5

Photo 4

Snip off the excess length of the new weaver on the inside of the shade. It is not necessary to trim the weaver length so precisely on pieces where the ends are not readily seen. In fact, leaving the new weaver a bit long is sometimes advantageous to the permanence of the repair.

Photo 5

This quick and easy repair does much to improve the appearance of this lamp shade.

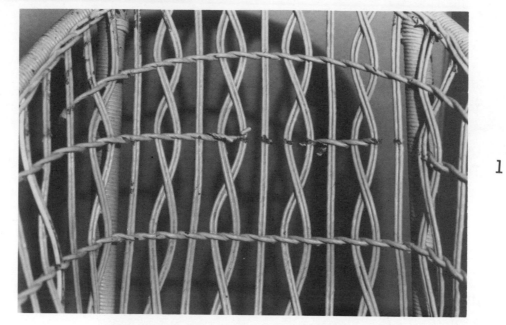

1

2

3

Replacing Pairing Weave

Photo 1

The pairing weave in open-weave furniture (widely spaced spokes and few weavers) holds the spokes in place and lends strength. Never piece a pairing weave but replace it in its entirety to retain the structural integrity of the furniture.

Photo 2

Allow extra length for the weavers. Duplicate the existing pattern keeping the braid snug as you proceed.

Photo 3

By replacing the pairing weave, this chair has regained its former strength and function.

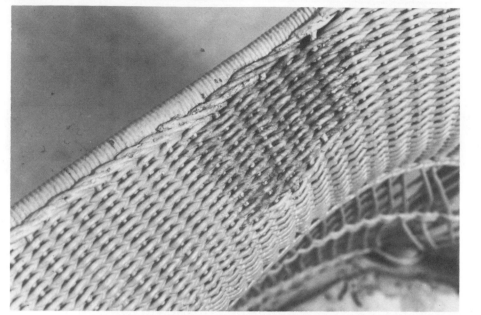

1

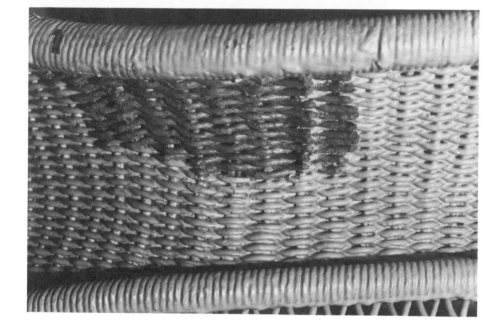

2

Mending a Hole

Photo 1

The arm on this sofa had missing and damaged weavers in an area approximately three by six inches. It would be impractical to replace the entire length of these weavers for they span the sofa from arm to arm for a distance of eight feet. Moreover, when painted, this repair will be undetectable except from the underside of the arm.

Photo 2

The replacement weavers project past the spokes underneath the arm about three eighths of an inch, providing extra insurance against slipping out of position. When weaving this area, leave the weavers long until they are all replaced. Then they can be cut off quickly and uniformly.

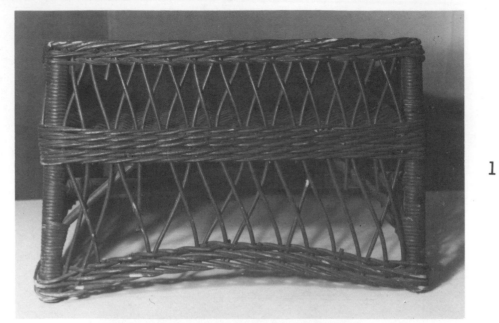

1

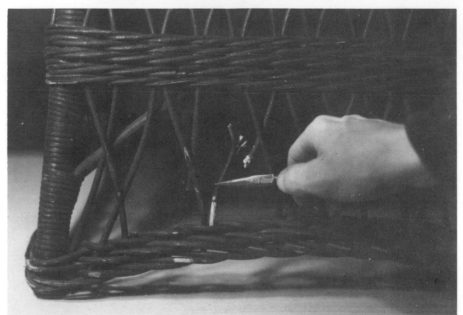

2

3

Spoke Replacement

Photo 1

The several broken spokes on this reed ottoman are easy to replace. These spokes support no weight (as do spokes in the back of a chair, for example) and therefore do not need to be replaced in their entirety to make a durable repair.

Photo 2

Cut off the top of the damaged spoke with a utility knife so that the new spoke may be inserted one inch into the weavers.

Photo 3

Pull out the bottom half of the damaged spoke. Needle nose pliers are handy for this. In this case, the spoke does not need to be cut on the bottom end because it merely sticks through the weavers and is not otherwise attached. Now remove the damaged top half of the spoke.

4

5

6

Photo 4

Insert a length of reed into the bottom rows of weavers.

Photo 5

Gently bend the reed and insert it into the top rows of weavers. The new spoke should touch the end of the old spoke above it. Check to see that the new spoke is parallel to the other spokes that go in the same direction, thus matching the existing pattern.

When replacing many spokes, you may desire to remove and replace one spoke at a time; to remove all broken spokes first makes it more difficult to duplicate the original pattern.

Photo 6

Finished repair.

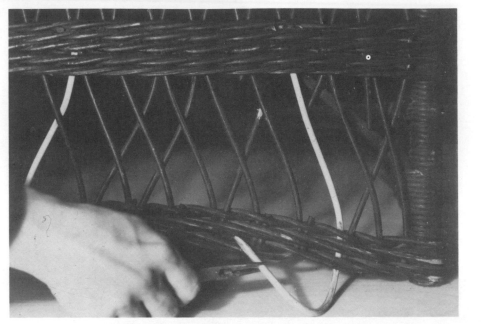

1

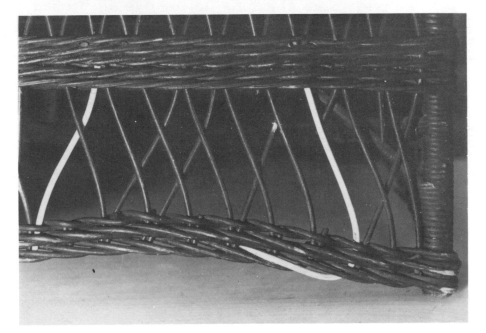

2

Spoke Continues as Part of Braid

Photo 1

In this example, the original spoke continues down through the bottom rows of weavers and is woven into the last couple of rows to make a braid. The top half of the broken spoke is removed as described in the preceding sequence. The bottom half of the broken spoke should first be studied to see how it is woven into the rows of weavers. The particular weaving sequence for this illustrated repair is not described in detail because there are numerous types of weaves employed in wicker. Careful observation will help you to duplicate the correct weaving pattern for your particular piece.

Now that you understand the pattern for weaving the bottom half of the spoke, take a piece of reed and insert it onto the upper rows of weavers, down through the bottom rows of weavers and into the proper pattern. Use diagonal cutters to trim off the excess reed on the inside of the furniture.

Photo 2

Finished repair.

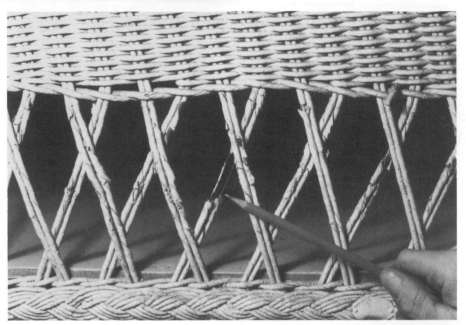

Substituting Reed for Fiber Rush

The more solidly built pieces of wicker furniture made from fiber rush have spokes composed of wire covered by fiber rush. This wire adds strength where it is needed most, as in the weight-bearing spokes on a couch or chair, for example. Fiber rush with a wire core is not readily available today so there are two choices: either use plain fiber rush where strength is not necessary, or, if strength is required, substitute reed. On a painted piece of wicker made of fiber rush, the reed replacement will be unnoticeable.

Photo 1

Due to weathering from repeated exposure to rain, the fiber rush has weakened and fallen off in spots on these spokes exposing the wire core. Note the use of spokes in pairs.

Photo 2

This is the bottom back of a sofa and the replacement spokes should go in approximately two inches into the weavers. Use diagonal cutters to snip the damaged spokes. Because the adjacent spokes are sound there is no need to extend the replacement spokes any further up into the weavers for strength.

3

4

Photo 3

Remove the braid on the frame of the sofa so the bad spokes can be detached.

Photo 4

Insert the new reed spokes and attach on the edge of the frame. Reattach the braid to complete the repair.

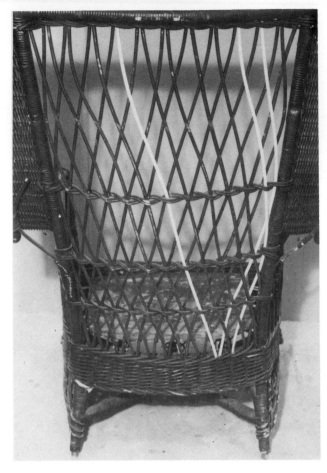

1

2

Replacing Spokes in Entirety

Photo 1

The spokes in the back of this chair are weight-bearing; therefore, any broken spokes must be replaced in their entirety to maintain the strength of the chair back.

Photo 2

Most of the spokes in the magazine rack on this armchair were broken. To maintain the structural integrity of the rack, the broken spokes had to be completely replaced.

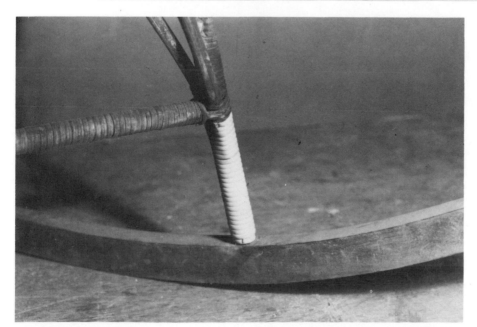

Wrapping with Cane

Photo 1

Remove all damaged wrapping and fasten any loose ends with a staple or brad in an inconspicuous location.

Photo 2

The wrapping on this chair is cane which often splits when nailed close to the end, therefore, leave an extra couple of inches when nailing. The new wrapping may be secured over the top of the old wrapping. After nailing, the cane can be trimmed close to the nail. A staple which just straddles the width of the cane is well suited here because it will not split the cane.

Photo 3

Continue wrapping until the repair is completed. Fasten in an inconspicuous place and trim off the excess cane. On this chair, the fasteners are located on the inside of the leg.

Wrapping with Fiber Rush

The woven material on this piece of furniture is fiber rush. Because of the thickness of the fiber rush, the new wrapping is not overlapped but is butt jointed to the old. Note the placement of the staples, especially those at the tip of the leg which keep the wrapping from slipping off. Also noteworthy is the use of two pieces of wrapping material at once.

Wooden Wedges Aid in Wrapping

To facilitate wrapping in a case such as this fernery, I have fashioned two simple wooden wedges which, when used on either side of the damaged area, allow me to have both hands free to make the repair.

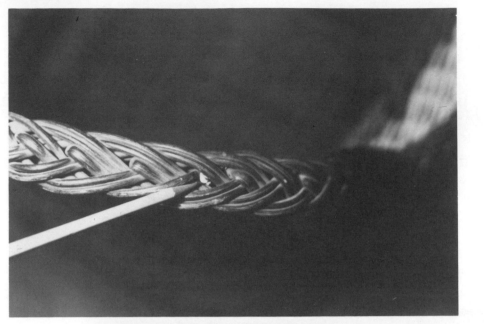

1

2

3

Piecing Braid

Photo 1

The braid on this reed chair is in excellent condition save for a few broken pieces.

Photo 2

Cut off each end of the broken reed where it will not show from the top side. Whenever possible cut from underneath: in this case it is not possible. You will want to provide a concealed notch for holding the replacement piece of reed.

Photo 3

Push one end of the reed in either notch as far as it will go.

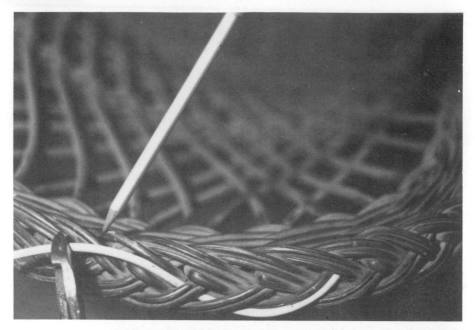

4

5

Photo 4

Weave the reed into the existing pattern. Cut reed to length allowing for the end to project fully into the other notch.

Photo 5

When this piece of reed is stained or painted it will match the original braid.

Making Braid

When damage to portions of the braid is extensive, it is best to make all new braid as this is the easiest and quickest method and produces the best looking results. Lengths of braid may be made from either reed or fiber rush. Of the two, reed is the more difficult to weave into a braid because of breakage. When restoring unpainted reed furniture, reed must, of necessity, be used for the replacement braid; however, fiber rush is an easy material to braid and when painted is virtually indistinguishable from painted reed.

The damaged braid provides the pattern (number of weavers in each group, number of groups, and over and under sequence) and when studied will show you how to weave matching replacement braid. Being able to make braid is also invaluable for covering the edge of replacement table tops (see the section on "Replacing a Table Top," p. 118).

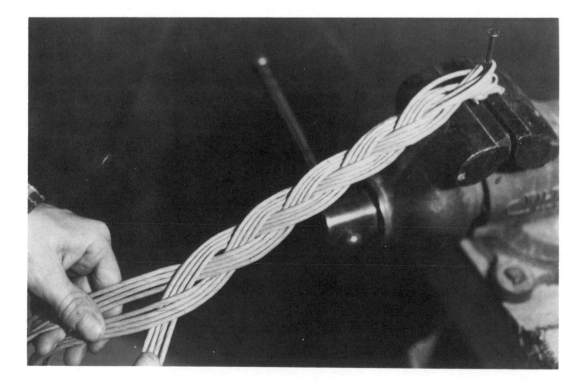

Choose the type and diameter of material, number and length of strands, and secure the ends in a vise or tie around any stationary object such as a nail pounded into a bench top. Allow excess length for the weavers: if a piece of braid needs to be six feet long when completed it may take weavers eight feet long. Err on the long side.

The braid in the photo is very simple to make as it is composed of only three groups of weavers. If you need braid for the edge of a table top and there is no other braid to be matched, this braid would be a good choice as it is attractive, simple to make, and is of a style often used on wicker. When choosing a style of braid there are two basic considerations: First, normally use weavers of the same diameter as that of the other weavers, and, secondly, the number of weavers used in each group should be such that the completed braid is of the proper width to cover the table edge. To achieve this, experiment with short weavers until the proper number is determined. Then use the correct length of weavers to make the braid.

Replacing a Section of Braid

If the damage is confined to a small section, braid can be made separately and woven into the existing braid. The ends of the new braid should be tacked or stapled under the old braid.

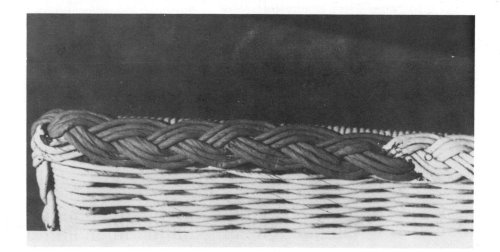

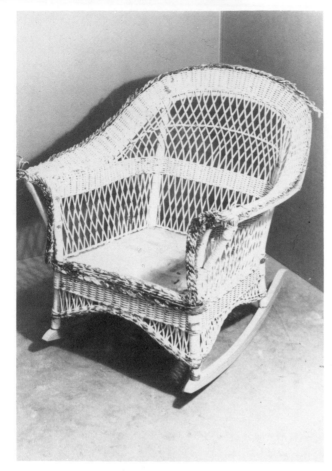

1

2

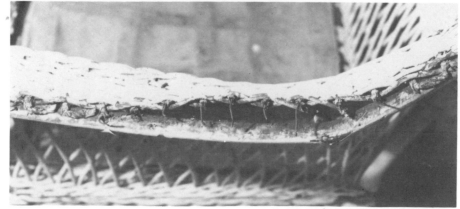

3

Replacing Entire Length of Braid

Photo 1

The braid on this chair is heavily damaged in numerous areas and entirely missing for over two feet on the arm. Making all new braid will be faster and easier than repairing the existing braid and will result in a more attractive repair.

Photo 2

Remove the old braid with a tack lifter. Save an end of the braid, as you will use this later. The rest of the braid may be discarded.

Photo 3

With the old braid removed, the need for reattaching the spokes to the framework becomes obvious.

4

5

6

Photo 4

These spokes are identical in outward appearance to the fiber rush available today with the notable exception of a wire core for strength. Spokes are quickly and securely fastened with a staple gun and narrow staples. After stapling, fold the end of the spoke back over the staple for extra security. Tacks or brads may also be used. Drive the tack in three-quarters of the way, wrap the wire around the shank of the tack to keep it from slipping, and drive the tack in completely. Continue until all spokes are securely attached.

Photo 5

Make braid following the directions given in the preceding section. Start attaching braid on the front post of the chair. Attach the ends of the braid following the same method employed on the original braid. Use the damaged sample as a pattern. Tack or staple the braid every three or four inches.

Photo 6

Braid completely attached.

Notes on Frame Repair

The framework on a piece of wicker furniture is the supporting foundation. When repairing framework that is not broken but merely loose or wobbly, it is often best to employ the same methods originally used in the construction.

A notable exception to this rule is in the use of nails. Nails were often used to join two members of the frame together. This was an easy but poor construction technique as nails work loose over the years. In these cases, remove the nails and replace them with screws.

A wood to wood joint with glue and dowels when properly executed is a stronger and longer lasting repair than one made with mechanical fasteners such as chair braces, angle irons, etc., but mechanical fasteners are sometimes the only practical solution when it is too difficult or time consuming to disassemble the piece of furniture to get to the framework joints.

Note the unsightly repair pictured below. Whoever attempted to repair this chair probably toiled long and hard to add the angle iron and wire brace and finally wrap the whole mess with some sort of coated wire. If this person had just taken the time to understand the basic framework of the chair, he would have been able to replace four nails quickly and easily with four screws, letting the original braces do the job for which they were intended, and to complete a lasting repair.

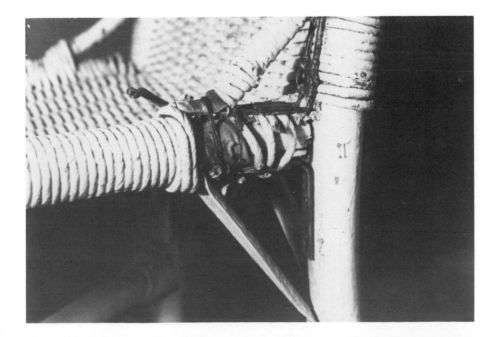

Tightening Existing Braces

This is a view of the bracing underneath a chaise lounge. Bracing of this type is common under many pieces of wicker. This chaise is slightly wobbly because the nails holding the metal braces have loosened over the years. All the nails should be removed and screws put in their places as has been done on the upper end of the brace. A small tack lifter is excellent for removing the nails.

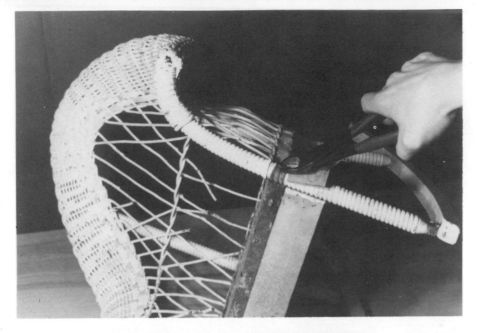

1

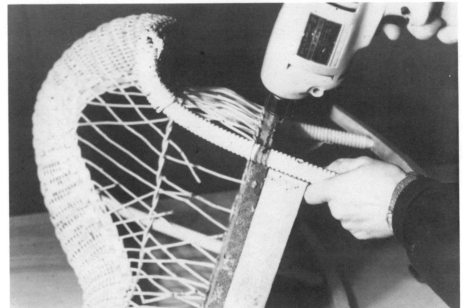

2

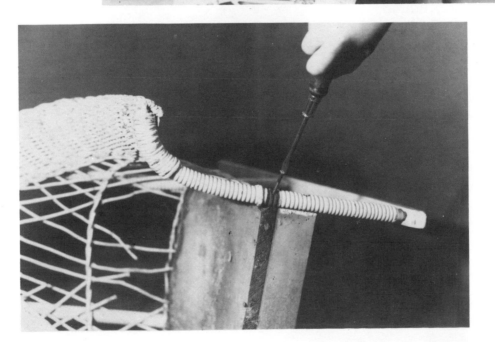

3

Tightening Joints on Frame by Replacing
Loose Nails with Screws

Photo 1

Remove nail holding joint together. Place scrap of wood underneath tool to prevent marring surfaces.

Photo 2

Drill a properly sized hole for the screw.

Photo 3

Put in screw.

1

2

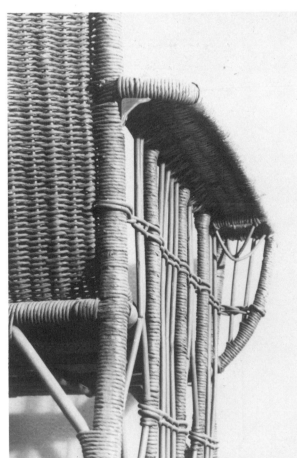

3

Frame Repair Using Chair Braces

Photo 1

The rear of this chair arm sags badly because the joint where the arm joins the back post is loose. This joint was originally held together with just a nail. It is very difficult to get to this joint with the woven back in place to replace the nail with a screw.

Photo 2

The proper solution, and the easiest one, is to attach a chair brace thereby eliminating a nailed joint and adding bracing. Push the arm back into its proper place, place a chair brace in position, drill holes for screws, and attach. The arm is once again attractive and even sturdier than it was originally.

Photo 3

From normal viewing height the chair brace is only visible from behind. The brace can be made even less conspicuous by either painting it the color of the chair or, if the chair is stained, using artists' acrylic paint to match the color. Chair braces are also available in a bronze tone which will match most stained furniture.

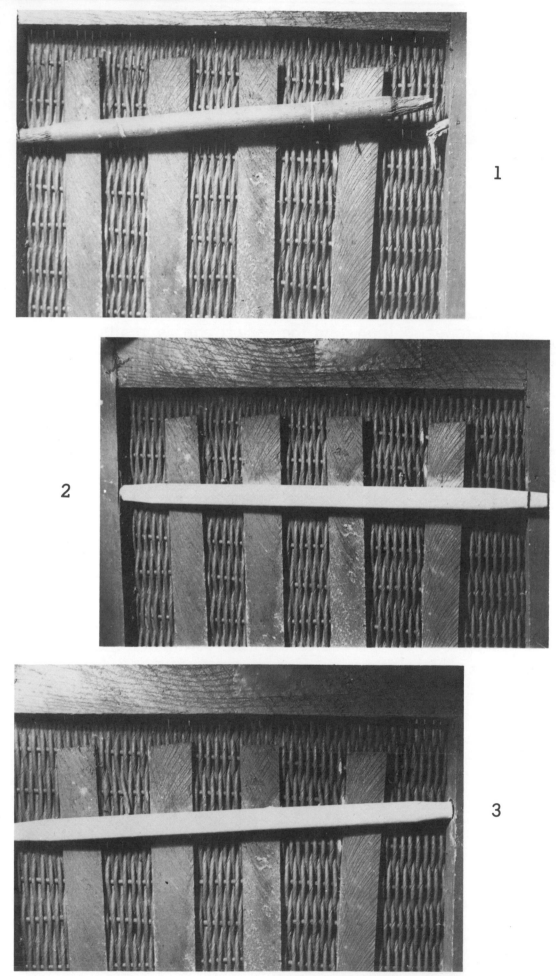

Broken Dowel Under Seat

Photo 1

The seat of this sofa is supported by thin slats running the length of the seat, the slats being supported in turn by dowels traversing the width of the seat (front to back). Without these supporting members the seat would likely break, so it is imperative to correct the broken dowel. To glue the dowel at the break would be ineffective—it would soon break again. Instead, we will replace it.

Photo 2

Remove the old dowel and select a hardwood dowel of the same diameter but longer. In this case, the dowel was tapered on the ends to fit into the holes in the frame. Sand or rasp the ends of the replacement dowel so that they will fit snugly into the holes after the holes have been scraped clean of any old glue. Push one end of the dowel into the hole in the frame as far as it will go. Now, mark the other end of the dowel so that after is it sawn it can be pushed into the other hole.

Photo 3

The dowel is now cut to length and ready for insertion into the hole. This is a test fit so no glue is used.

4

1

Photo 4

Push the dowel halfway into this second hole. Some additional sanding or rasping may be necessary to accomplish this. The dowel should fit tightly in both holes. Remove the dowel and put glue in both holes before reinserting. Drive a small brad about one-half inch long through the frame and into the dowel at one end to hold it in place while the glue dries.

Replacing Seat Support Slats

Wicker furniture with woven seats often had slats underneath for support, thus relieving some of the stress on the woven material.

Photo 1

Remove the broken slats and cut new slats of the same dimensions. The slat on the left is in the proper position. The right slat shows the method of insertion. Put the slat in as far as it will go on one side of the frame and at an angle to allow the slat to be pushed into correct position. When all slats are in the proper position, turn the piece right side up and with small brads nail the ends of the slats to the frame to hold them in place. Gently pry the weavers apart to make the nailing easier.

1

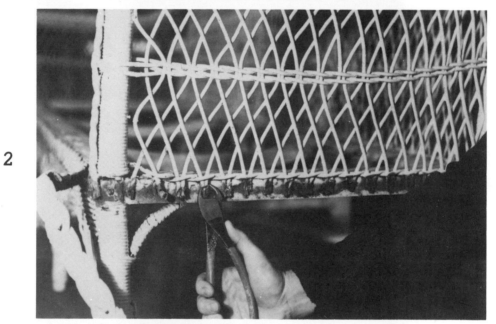

2

3

Repairing a Broken Post or Leg

Photo 1

The front post of this sofa is broken where the seat and the post meet. This break is not easily seen yet it extends across the entire diameter of the post. Gently wiggling the sofa arm to check for sturdiness uncovered this flaw. This same repair technique may be used to mend a broken leg.

Photo 2

Remove the braid to make the repair area accessible. The braid encompassing this sofa is one continuous length wrapped around the sofa. The ends of the braid join on the back corner of the sofa on the end with the broken post. Therefore, this point is the logical place to start removing the braid as it can be easily and inconspicuously reattached after the front post is repaired. If the braid ends do not join in a place near the damage, you will want to cut the braid with a utility knife in the most inconspicuous spot near the repair. It can be easily spliced if the cut is carefully and cleanly made.

Next, remove the brads holding the spokes to the seat frame. Enough spokes should be detached to allow the upper half of the sofa arm to be shifted to the side for drilling holes for a dowel; furthermore, the arm needs to be lifted when inserting the dowel, so detach plenty of spokes to give yourself working room.

Photo 3

Remove the nail holding the leg to the frame.

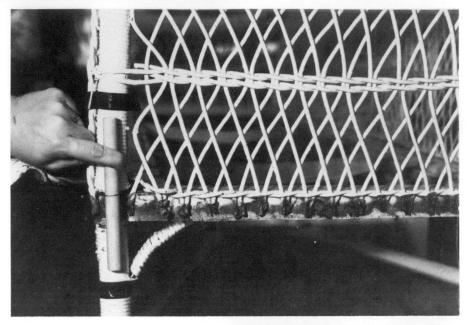

4

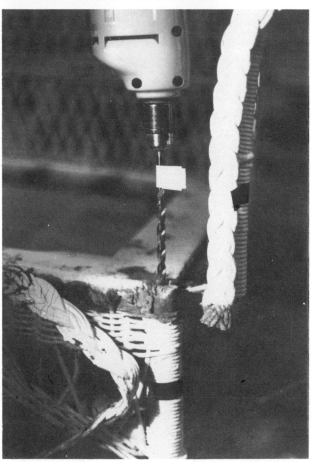

5

Photo 4

To help visualize this repair, the proper length and diameter of hardwood dowel is being held next to the post. The diameter of the post is one inch. A five-eighth inch diameter dowel has been chosen as most suitable for the repair: this provides a dowel large enough for strength while leaving enough of the original post wood intact around the dowel. The black tape indicates the depth of the holes to be drilled. A dark line is also scribed around the dowel equidistant from each end.

Photo 5

The top half of the post is pushed to one side. Any brads in the post that hold on braid, etc., are removed to eliminate drilling interference. It is easier to center the dowel hole if an undersized drill bit is used to drill a pilot hole. Note the tape on the drill bit indicating the proper depth for drilling. The hole is drilled to about one-half inch deeper than the dowel to be inserted, allowing space for excess glue. Next, enlarge this pilot hole to the proper size with a larger diameter drill bit. The hole should be just slightly larger in diameter than the dowel rod to provide room for glue and to allow for easier insertion. Repeat these operations on the top half of the broken post. Check the alignment of the dowel holes with a dry fit. Insert the dowel into the bottom half of the post until the scribed line on the dowel is level with the top of the hole. Then raise the top half of the post until it can be pushed over the dowel rod. If necessary, detach more spokes to accomplish this. Push down on the arm until the joint closes. Step back and check the alignment. Is the post in correct alignment with the rest of the chair when viewed from the front and the side? If so, proceed to the next step. If not, make any minor corrections. If the alignment is off considerably, analyze why, disassemble, cut the dowel in half and glue either or both halves in the incorrectly drilled holes to plug them, let dry overnight, and then start over with drilling.

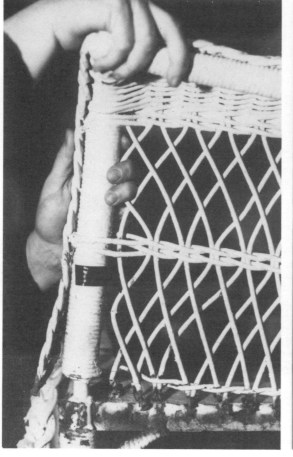

6

7

8

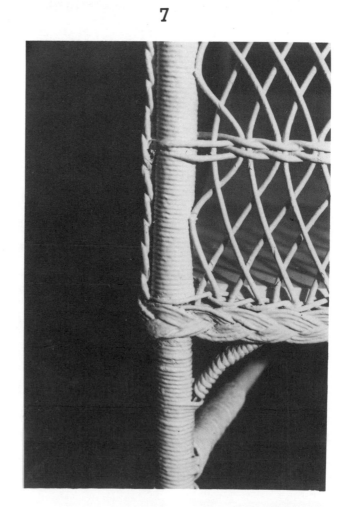

Photo 6

Coat the dowel hole with glue on the bottom half of the post and insert the dowel halfway. The scribed line on the dowel helps to indicate this. Coat the top half of the dowel with glue and push the arm down until the joint closes. Wipe off any excess glue and let the joint dry overnight.

Photo 7

Replace the nail that held the post to the seat frame with a screw. The hole through the post should be slightly larger in diameter than the shank of the screw to avoid splitting the post. Reattach the spokes and the braid.

Photo 8

Finished repair.

1

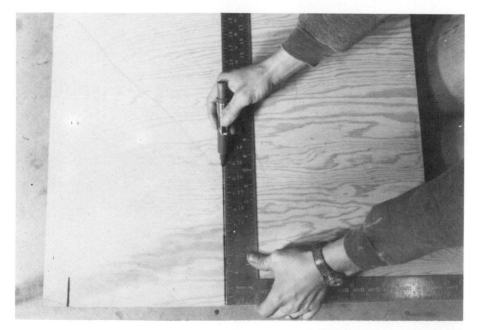

2

3

Plywood Foundation

An easy, inexpensive and satisfactory replacement for springs in furniture such as chairs and sofas is a plywood foundation for cushions. This technique also strengthens the frame and adds to the overall rigidity of the piece.

Photo 1

All nails, tacks, or staples should be removed from the top of the seat frame so that the plywood will sit flush on the frame.

Photo 2

The plywood used should be three-eighths inch thick with one good side (devoid of knot holes) to be used as the top side. Measure the width of the front of the chair seat including the front posts. The plywood will later be notched to fit within these posts. Subtract one inch from this total width: this allows a one-half inch border on each side facilitating easy fitting of the plywood. Transfer this measurement to the plywood. Before proceeding to step three, look at the rest of the photos. This will clarify the process.

Photo 3

Most chairs and sofas have seats which taper—they are wider at the front and narrower at the back. Establishing a center line on the plywood makes it easy to taper the sides of the plywood seat to a corresponding taper. Find the centerpoint between the marks you have made to designate the chair front. Use a square to scribe a line perpendicular from that centerpoint.

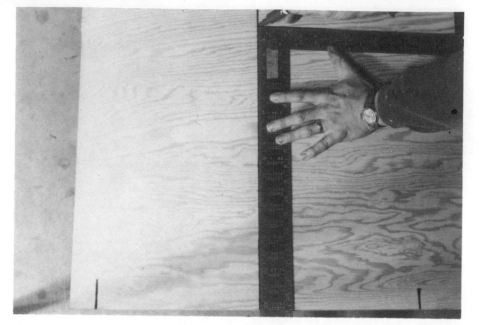

4

5

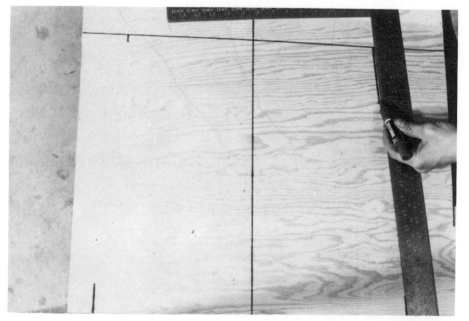

6

Photo 4

Measure the depth of the chair seat, subtract one inch, and mark this measurement on the perpendicular line. Use the square to draw another line designating the back of the seat. The front and back will, of course, be parallel and the perpendicular line marks the midpoint of both the seat front and back.

Photo 5

Measure the width of the seat at the back of the chair including the posts. Again, subtract one inch from this measurement. Mark this width on the plywood with half of the width on either side of the perpendicular line, thus centering the back of the seat.

Photo 6

With the use of a straightedge, mark the tapered sides.

7

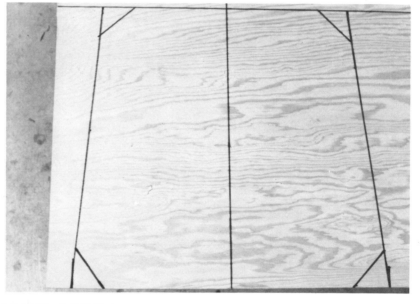

8

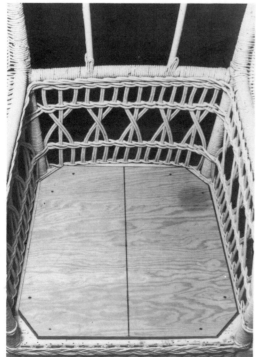

9

Photo 7

Mark notching of all corners. If desired, corners may be cut to fit the contour of the posts.

Photo 8

With all marking completed, the plywood is ready to be cut. All the edges should be sanded.

Photo 9

Put plywood on seat frame and mark where screws will attach the plywood to the seat frame.

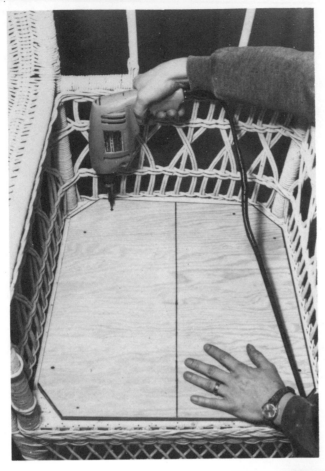

10

11

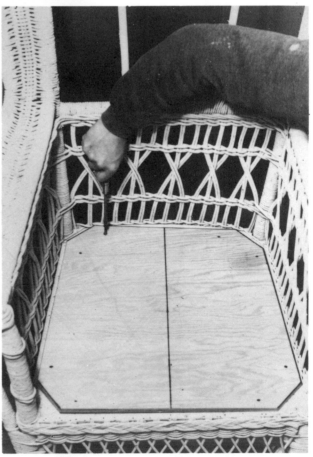

Photo 10

Drill holes for screws with the plywood in place. The holes should be countersunk in the plywood so that the screw heads are slightly below the surface.

Photo 11

Attach the plywood with screws. In most cases, the edges of the plywood cannot be easily seen when a cushion is in place. If the edges are visible, a fabric cover can be installed over the plywood.

1

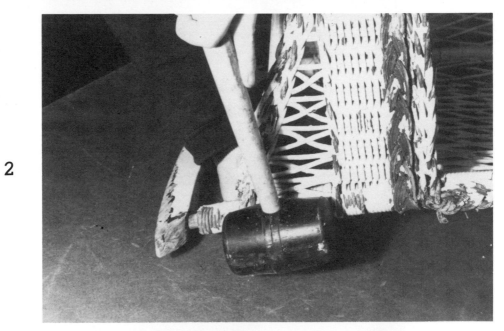

2

3

Repairing Loose Runner on Rocking Chair

Photo 1

Check first for small brads through the sides of the runner into chair legs. Remove any brads.

Photo 2

Tap the runner off with a rubber mallet. The part of the chair leg that fits into the hole (mortise) in the runner is called the tenon.

Photo 3

Use a wood rasp or rough sandpaper to remove the old glue from the leg tenons. Try to remove as little wood as possible. Also, scrape the old glue from the mortise in the runner. Now is the time to sand the old finish off the runner and to get it in good condition for new paint or varnish.

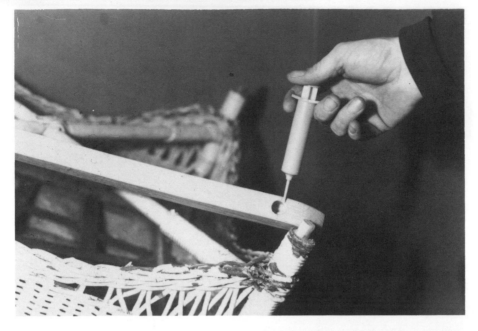

4

5

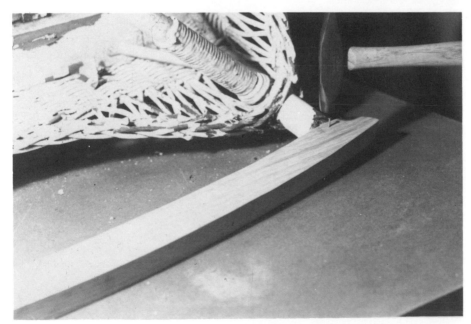

6

Photo 4

Put Franklin Home and Craft® glue in both mortises in the runner.

Photo 5

Place the rocking chair on its side and gently tap the runner on with a rubber mallet. Some excess glue should squeeze from the brad hole and from around the mortise, indicating that the joint is sufficiently coated. Wipe off the excess glue with a sponge or rag and warm water.

Photo 6

Pound in the small brads. Allow the glue to dry overnight before using.

1

2

3

Replacing Broken Tenon on Rocking Chair

Photo 1

The tenon of the leg of this rocking chair has broken off and needs to be replaced before the runner can be reattached.

Photo 2

Select a hardwood dowel the same diameter as the broken tenon. Drill a hole in the leg to receive this dowel. It is easiest to center this hole if a small diameter drill bit is first used to drill a pilot hole. Next, use the proper diameter drill bit for the hardwood dowel. Masking tape on the drill bit marks the depth.

Photo 3

Cut the dowel to the proper length: it should seat fully in the hole in the leg and project enough to fill the mortise. Apply glue to the hole in the leg and tap in the dowel. Then, attach the runner as described in the preceding section.

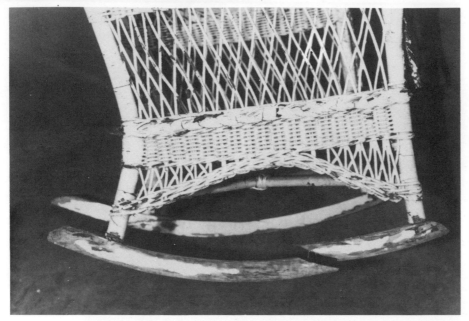

1

2

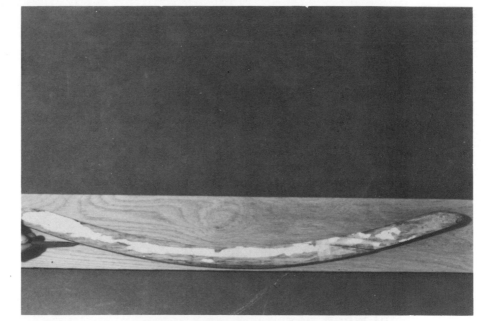

3

Replacing Runners on Rocking Chair

Photo 1

Both runners on this rocking chair are bad and need to be replaced. Most often breaks in runners cannot be satisfactorily glued. Remove the nails holding the runners to the leg tenons and tap the runners off. (Refer to photos 1 and 2 in "Repairing Loose Runner on Rocking Chair," p. 82.)

Photo 2

Lay the old runner on a hardwood board of the same thickness and trace the outline.

Photo 3

Place the board with the runner outline on top of another suitable board and nail them together using one nail at each end of the runner pattern. Drill pilot holes for the nails to avoid splitting the boards. Thus stacked, two runners of identical shape are cut using a bandsaw, jigsaw, or coping saw. Always saw to the outside, or waste side, of the line. This leaves a reference point useful when next sanding away the saw marks. The runners can be clamped together for sanding.

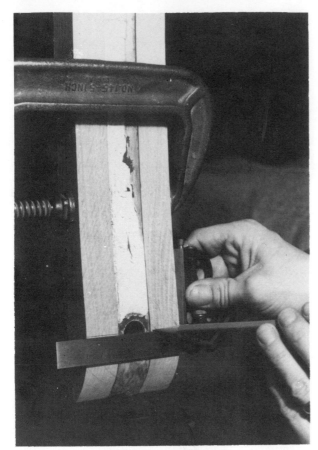

4

5

6

Photo 4

Clamp the new runners and the old runner together. Use a try square and scribe a line across the runners indicating the center of the mortises to be drilled in the new runners.

Photo 5

Mark the center point of each line so the mortises will be drilled in the center of the runners.

Photo 6

The new mortises should be drilled to the same diameter and depth as the old mortises. Place a drill bit of the proper diameter in the old mortise and use masking tape as a depth stop.

7

8

9

Photo 7

Insert a dowel section in the mortise in the bad runner to serve as a guide for drilling the new mortises. Keep the drill bit parallel with the dowel rod and the resulting mortise will fit on the leg tenon properly. Drill all mortises in this manner.

Photo 8

Mark and drill brad holes on the inside edge of the runners using the old runner as a model for hole placement. Glue and attach runners as described in photos 3 through 6 in the section on "Repairing Loose Runner on Rocking Chair," p. 82-85.

Photo 9

Finished runners installed.

1

2

3

Reattaching Scrollwork

Photo 1

The scrollwork on this buggy is intact; however, the brads have worked loose over the years and need to be replaced.

Photo 2

Because of the delicate nature of scrollwork, it is often difficult to use a hammer to drive in brads. I have found VISE-GRIP® pliers to be invaluable for squeezing the brads into place.

Photo 3

Finished repair.

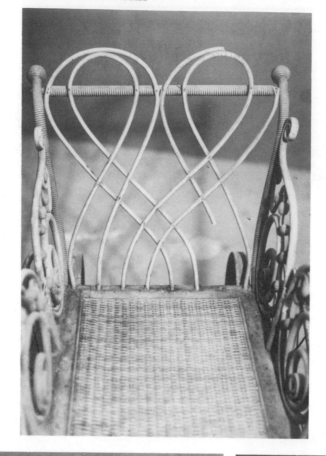

1

2

3

Replacing Scrollwork

Photo 1

The scrollwork on this Victorian buggy is comprised of several loops of round reed. To repair the broken section, it is best to replace one entire loop. This is the easiest, strongest, and most attractive repair method.

Photo 2

Study the pattern of the reed. Start at the frame when beginning the repair. Remove the old reed and glue from the hole in the frame where the loop of reed starts. Put glue in the hole and insert the end of the new reed and follow the pattern of the broken reed, removing nails holding the old reed in place and replacing with new nails as the repair progresses. The broken reed could all be removed before the insertion of the replacement reed if the pattern is easy to follow. The new reed is left extra long.

Photo 3

Cut the reed to proper length, clean the hole in the frame and apply glue. Insert the reed to complete the repair.

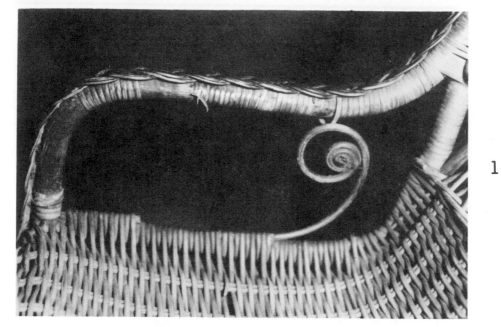

1

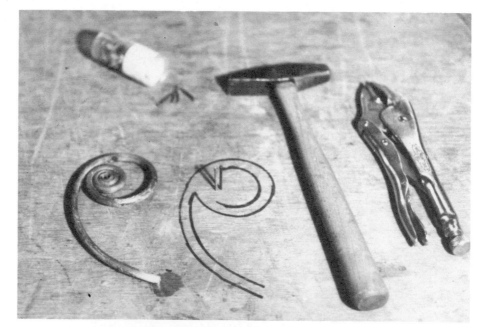

2

3

Making Scrollwork

Photo 1

The scrollwork found on many early reed pieces is what contributes to the ornate, Victorian look that appeals to many collectors. Ranging from simple, broad loops to complex and coiled curlicues, scrollwork is highly decorative and also susceptible to damage. As you can see, one of the pieces of scrollwork is missing from the side of this chair.

Photo 2

The missing scrollwork was identical to the piece remaining on the chair. To make duplication easiest, the scrollwork on the chair is carefully removed to serve as a pattern. Trace the outline of this piece on a board. A hammer, brads, and a pair of VISE-GRIP® pliers should be ready at hand. Drive two finishing nails into the board at the center of the marked scrollwork pattern. Leave just enough room between the nails to wedge the tapered end of a length of reed. The beginning (or inside loop) of a coil of this type is usually tapered for approximately two inches. The reed should be soaked long enough to be extremely pliable. Allow plenty of reed for ease in bending and attaching to the chair.

Photo 3

Insert the tapered end of the reed between the two nails. Slowly and deliberately bend the reed to conform to the pattern. The pliers are often helpful in compressing the reed to the desired circumference.

4

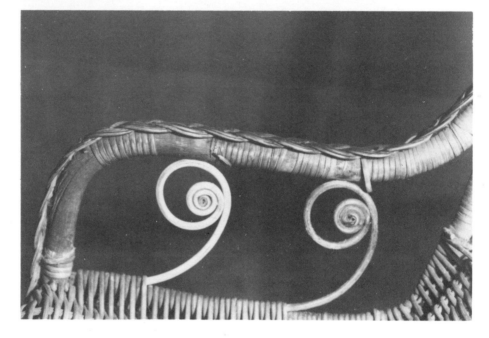

5

Photo 4

After the reed is coiled to match the pattern, insert a brad to hold the coils together. The brad may be driven with a hammer or squeezed into place with pliers. Remove the finishing nails holding the scrollwork to the board and attach the piece to the chair.

Photo 5

The new scrollwork is now attached.

Notes on Serpentine Repair

Serpentine arms are one of the most beautiful and graceful elements of wicker furniture; however, these parts are often damaged because of the great stress put upon them over the years. The key to successful repair of serpentine parts is in the spoke replacement: once this is properly done, the rest of the repair is easy. This is one of the most satisfying of repairs and provides very dramatic results.

1

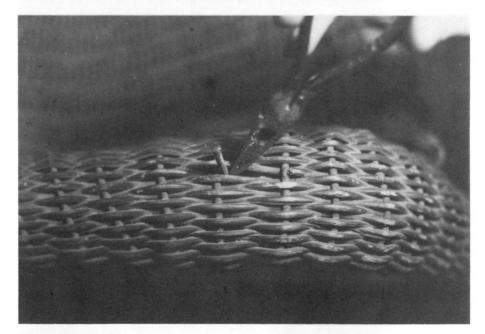

2

3

Piecing Weavers on Serpentine Arm

Photo 1

Replacing a damaged weaver on a serpentine arm presents the problem of how to cut off the ends of the damaged weaver.

Photo 2

If the weaver is reed, it is best to snap off the end of the damaged weaver with the tip of a pair of needle nose pliers. If the weaver is fiber rush in poor condition (dry and brittle), this same technique will work, but if the fiber rush is in good condition, pull the damaged end out, estimate where it goes under the spoke (this can be seen by the curve the material has permanently taken on from being woven in such a pattern for a length of time), cut at this spot and reinsert.

Photo 3

Insert the new weaver leaving it long on each end approximately one inch. This extra length will not show and helps to further lock the weaver in place.

4

5

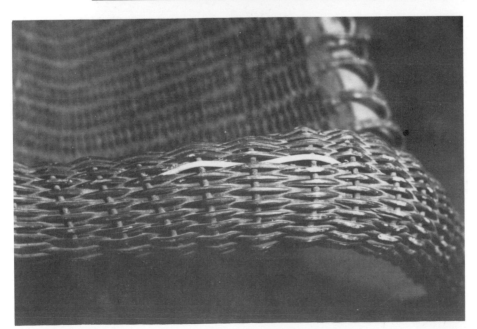

6

Photo 4

The finished repair. This technique generally works well with reed but if the replacement weaver seems too loose, follow the instructions illustrated in the following two photos.

Photo 5

Snap off the old weaver one spoke over and, starting with a new piece of reed, weave the replacement weaver over and under two spokes for a secure weave. This technique is especially recommended when the repair calls for fiber rush because fiber rush does not "spring back" and lock itself like reed.

Photo 6

The finished repair.

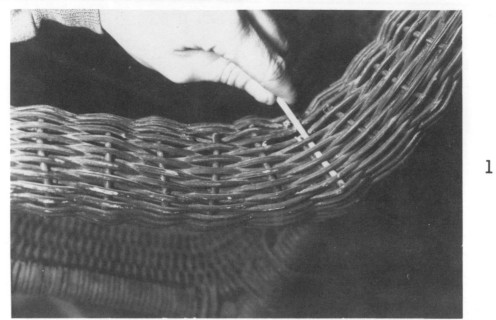

1

2

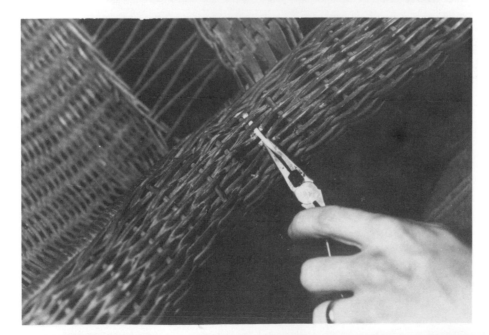

3

Piecing Spokes on Serpentine Arm

Photo 1

The arm of this chair is in good condition except for a few spokes broken on the top of the arm. I use a piecing technique that satisfactorily bridges the broken gap and provides strength by placing a partial spoke alongside the broken one.

First, run an ice pick alongside the broken spoke on both sides of the gap to gently push the spoke to one side making room for the new spoke.

Push in a length of reed. The reed should be pushed in a distance as long as the gap plus two inches. When the repair is completed, the new spoke will not only bridge the gap, but will extend one inch on each side of the gap.

Photo 2

Cut off the new spoke where it will enter alongside the broken spoke on the other side of the gap.

Photo 3

Insert the new reed next to the old spoke and use pliers to push it alongside to a depth of one inch to complete the repair.

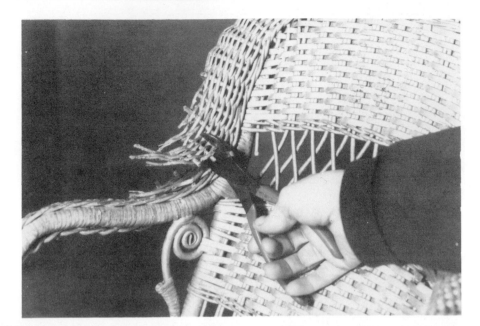

1

2

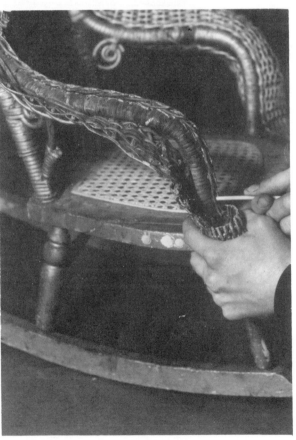

3

Replacing Serpentine Arm

Photo 1

Trim off all broken weavers up to the first sound spoke at the top end of the repair area. Do the same with the bottom end of the repair area. Removing all of these broken pieces first makes it easier to work and to see what needs to be done. There is no need to remove any weavers that are unbroken. Note: as can be seen in photo 3, the underside of the arm is not removed even though the spokes are not continuous. There are two reasons for this: first, the remaining weavers are sound and portions of the spokes are still firmly glued in their sockets, thereby providing an excellent foundation for repairing the missing portion of the arm, and, secondly, the underside of the arm does not show unless the chair is turned upside down. Naturally, if the underside of the arm were not sound it would also be replaced, but I have found in my practice that few serpentine arms need to be replaced all the way around.

Photo 2

Now we are ready to replace the spokes. Sometimes the old spokes can be removed by merely pulling them out with needle nose pliers. In this photo there are stubs still firmly glued in place on the top of the arm so they must be drilled out. Select a drill bit of the same diameter as the spoke. Drill out each broken spoke on the top edge of the arm to a depth of one half inch. Wrap masking tape around the drill bit to serve as a depth stop.

Photo 3

Put a small amount of Franklin Titebond® glue into the spoke hole. Select a piece of reed of the proper diameter and a few inches longer than seems necessary. This reed should be soaked for several minutes until it is extremely pliable. Insert the reed into the hole. A small amount of glue should squeeze out indicating the reed is adequately glued. If not, remove the reed and put in more glue.

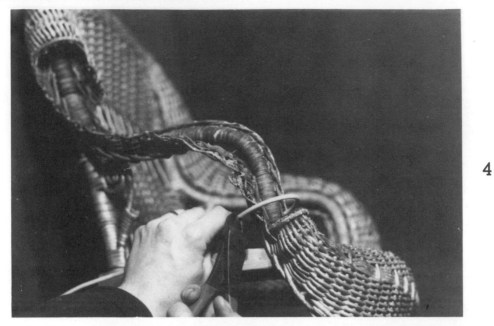

4

5

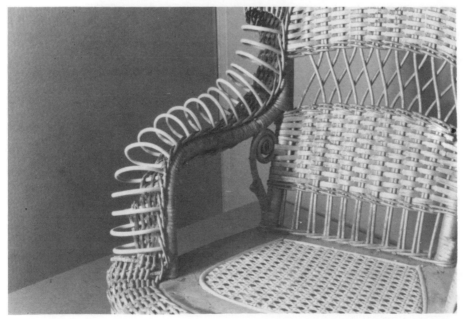

6

Photo 4

Bend the spoke to duplicate the curvature of the adjacent spoke. Cut off the spoke so that when fully inserted into the underside of the arm alongside the remaining piece of old spoke this curvature is maintained. Carefully observe the graceful curve of the arm you are replacing. Often, as in this case, the other arm will serve as a model. Every spoke is slightly different in height to create this smooth curve. Therefore, every reed used in this repair will differ somewhat in length. After several spokes are put in place it is easier to visualize this. If you find you have any spokes the wrong height, simply replace them.

Photo 5

Insert the spoke into the underside of the arm alongside the old spoke. Leave the remainder of the old spoke as it does not show and adds to the strength of the repair. No glue is necessary here.

Photo 6

Methodically replace all spokes. Double check the outline of this curve to ensure that the arms match. Let the spokes dry in place overnight.

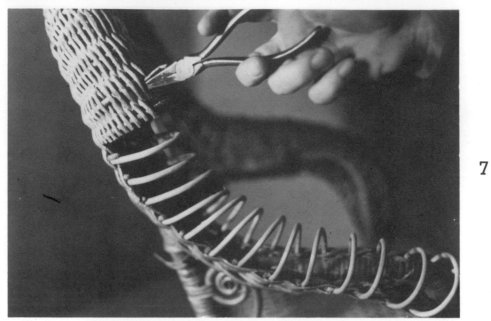

7

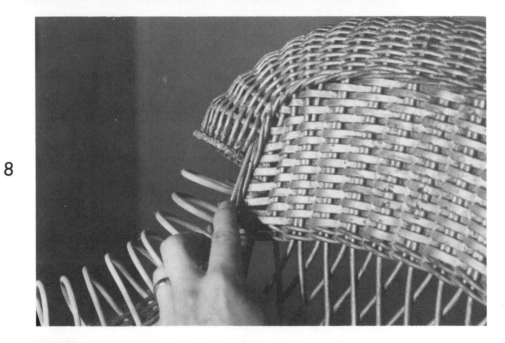

8

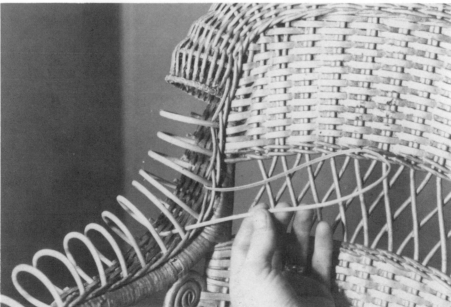

9

Photo 7

Use the needle nose pliers to break off the weavers that come over the top of the last spoke. These weavers should be broken off so that they end under the next spoke. In other words, all of the old weavers should end underneath a spoke. Do this at both ends of the repair section.

Photo 8

Insert the end of a new weaver under the end of an old weaver. Let the new end project into the chair arm about one inch past the end of the old weaver. This ensures that the new weaver will not pop out. This projection, since it is on the inside of the arm, will not show when the arm is completed. Since you started <u>under</u> a spoke weave <u>over</u> the next one.

Photo 9

Repeat this over and under pattern until the new weaver passes underneath the old weaver at the other end of the repair. Again, let the new weaver project about one inch past the end of the old weaver.

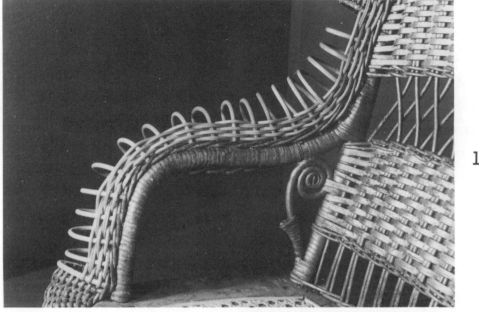

10

11

Photo 10

Several of the new weavers are now in place. This picture shows unequal spacing between some of the spokes. This is not a result of careless restoration: the replacement spokes have the same spacing as the original spokes. The original spokes were simply not evenly spaced. Continue inserting new weavers until the arm is complete.

Photo 11

Finished chair.

Replacing a Table Top

Damaged table tops are common on old wicker furniture. Sometimes the damage may be repaired by regluing loose veneer. Holes and deep scratches may be filled with wood putty. If the damage is major, however, it is best to replace the top.

A new top may be made by gluing several boards together to make a top of the desired width. This technique, coupled with careful craftsmanship and the proper selection of boards, can result in a beautiful top. The appearance can be further enhanced by shaping or molding the edge. Instructions for building this type of top are best found in a book on cabinet making and furniture construction.

The majority of wicker tables were constructed with veneered tops. Hardwood plywood (plywood with surface veneers of birch, oak, walnut, etc.) is available today for restoring tops. I find this material very valuable because it eliminates the need for gluing individual boards, resists warping and splitting, and is available in 4'x8' sheets.

Photo 1

When a top is in this condition it is best to replace it with a new one.

Photo 2

The braid around the edge of the table top is in good condition. Therefore, it will be saved for putting around the replacement top. With a small tack lifter, pry gently until the braid is lifted from the table edge about one quarter of an inch.

Photo 3

Push the braid back against the edge of the table to expose the heads of the brads attaching the braid. Use the tack lifter and a wooden back up block to remove the brads. The wooden block prevents the tack lifter from marring the braid. After removing all of the brads, lift off the braid and set it aside.

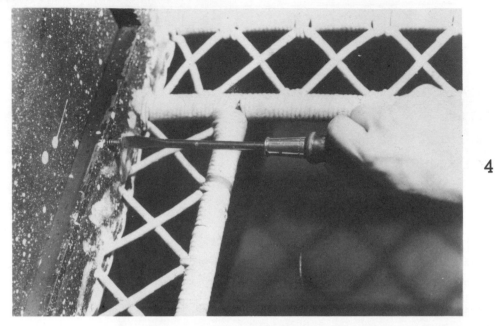

4

5

6

Photo 4

Remove the screws holding the table top to the base.

Photo 5

This photo illustrates how the top fits on the table base. The underneath of the table top is shown. It can also be seen that the braid, standing on end in front of the top, was taken off in one piece.

Use the old top as a pattern for making a replacement top. If the new top is to be cut from plywood, lay the old top on the plywood, trace the pattern and cut. Or, if desired, a larger or even differently shaped top may be cut. Regardless of the type saw blade used it should be very sharp to avoid splintering and, if a portable jigsaw is used, put masking tape on its base so it will not mar the face of the plywood.

Photo 6

Place the new top upside down on a pad and set the base on it. Center the base and mark the holes for the screws which hold the top to the base.

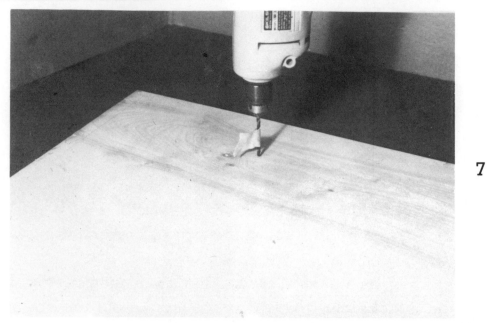

7

8

9

Photo 7

Drill holes in the underside of the top so that the base can be screwed to the top. Use tape as a depth stop on the drill bit to avoid drilling through the top.

Attach the new top with screws. Any sanding necessary on the top should be done now.

Photo 8

Place the table on edge on a pad and reattach the braid with brads.

Photo 9

The top is now ready for a finish. If the plywood top is to be painted, birch plywood is an excellent choice because it paints to a smooth surface. For a natural top—one finished with varnish or a penetrating oil finish—any hardwood plywood may be used, the sole criterion being aesthetic. These natural tops may be stained if desired. A natural top does not necessarily have to be joined to a natural base; in fact, a natural top on a painted base is quite striking. In these cases, the braid around the edge of the top is painted.

1

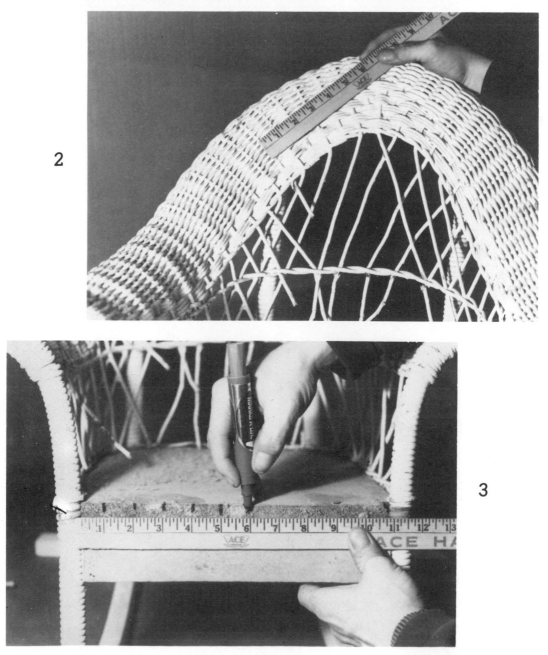

2

3

Skirt Replacement

Photo 1

The skirt, the woven material which covers the front of a chair below the seat, is missing from this child's rocker. Replacing a skirt is time consuming but not difficult.

Photo 2

To ensure that the replacement skirt will look like the original, measure the distance between the spokes on the back of the chair. This spoke interval would be the same as that used for the skirt.

Photo 3

Mark the spoke interval on the front of the chair. The spokes on either end should be the same distance from the inside of the front chair legs.

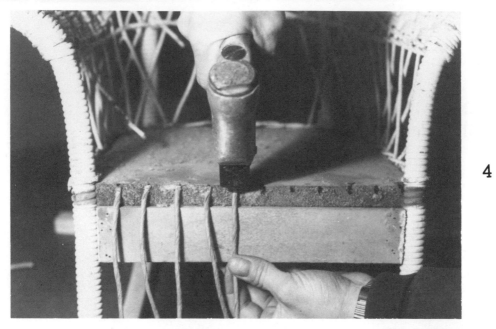

4

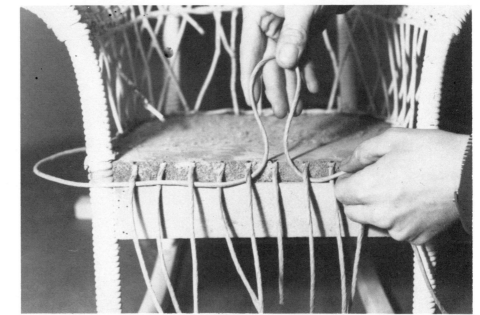

5

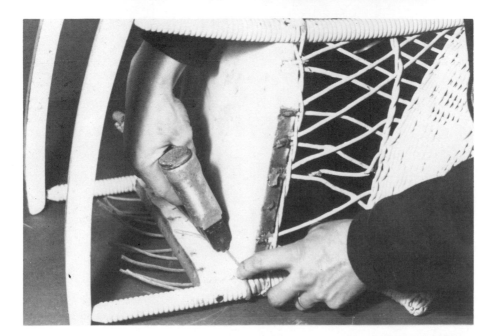

6

Photo 4

Attach the spokes to the front of the chair, leaving them long enough to wrap under the chair where they will be attached to the inside of the skirt board. Note: match the diameter of these new spokes with those used elsewhere in the chair.

Photo 5

Start inserting the weavers following the pattern used in the rest of the chair. Leave each end of the weaver long enough to allow for attaching two or three inches inside of the back of the skirt board. The object is to make the weavers long enough so their point of attachment is hidden from view. Also, the first weaver need only be within one-half inch of the top of the spoke as braid will cover this area.

Photo 6

Attach both ends of the weaver on the back of the skirt board.

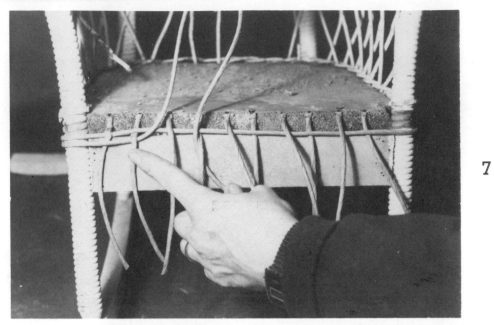

7

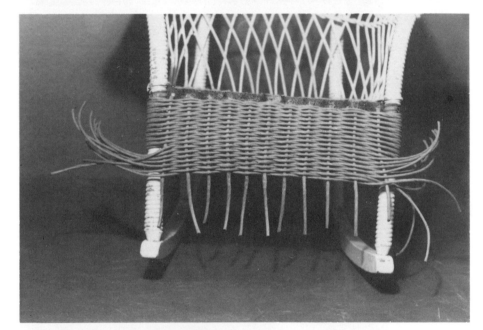

8

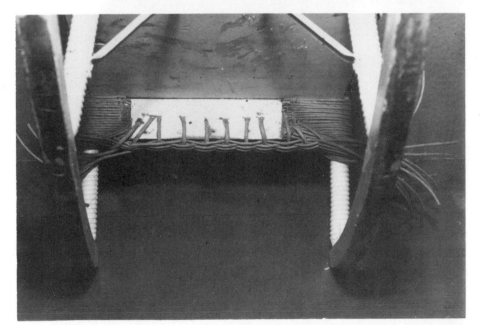

9

Photo 7

Put in the second weaver following the weave pattern used elsewhere in the chair.

Photo 8

Continue putting in weavers and attaching the ends until reaching the bottom of the skirt board. Next, add weavers without attaching their ends until the skirt extends approximately 1½ inches below the bottom of the skirt board. This extra length will be wrapped around the bottom of the board.

Photo 9

Trim the excess off the <u>attached</u> weavers. Wrap the skirt around the bottom of the board and attach the spokes on the back side of the skirt board.

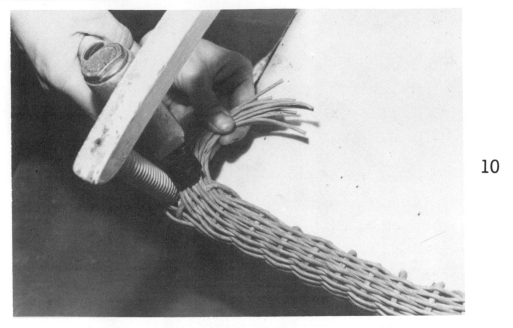

10

11

12

Photo 10

Gather the loose ends of the weavers and attach to the back side of the skirt board. Trim off the excess.

Photo 11

This is the finished skirt.

Photo 12

The finished skirt with braid attached.

1

2

3

Leaning Floor Lamp

Photo 1

Often the bases to floor lamps or birdcage stands lean, making them unattractive and in some cases useless. The floor lamp pictured was certainly in the latter category before repairs. The weaving is in good shape except for a few small broken spots.

Photo 2

The main problem causing the lamp to lean is the broken insert. The insert is not only broken but has a large section of wood missing from the center.

Photo 3

Remove all screws and nails holding the insert to the shaft of the lamp and to the woven part of the base. Gently lift out the wooden insert. If the segments of the insert are complete but merely separate because of loose glue joints, it is easy to clean off the old glue, reglue, and replace the old insert.

In the case illustrated, it is easiest to make a new insert using the original as a pattern. Also, now is the time to replace the old lamp cord. For safety's sake, the lamp cord should be replaced in its entirety, from lamp socket to the plug.

4

5

Photo 4

    The new insert is now in place. Three screws and glue hold it to the shaft of the lamp. The fit of this shaft into the hole on the inside of the insert should be snug. Further support is given by attaching the woven base to the insert with small brads or staples.

Photo 5

    The finished lamp is solidly upright and attractive.

Repair of a Woven Lamp Base

Before it was repaired, this base was very wobbly. The insert was in good condition but the woven material was bad. All the broken weavers were removed and the old spokes reattached to the insert. New spokes were installed, resulting in a sturdy base once more.

Notes on Caning

There are two types of caning used in chair seats and backs. One is hand woven: strands of cane are woven by hand through holes in the frame to form a desired pattern. Most of the suppliers on page 159 sell an instruction manual featuring this type of caning. The other type is called a pressed cane seat because the cane, woven into a sheet of the desired pattern by machine, is pressed or driven into a groove in the frame and glued and fastened with a piece of triangular reed called spline.

Below is a beautiful example of a chair featuring a hand woven back and seat.

1

2

Pressed Cane Seat Replacement

Photo 1

Remove all old spline from the groove. Both the outer and inner edges of the spline need to be separated from the groove. This can be accomplished by either tapping lightly with a chisel and mallet or by very carefully using a utility knife to score this area. Next, use a narrow chisel to pry the spline from the groove. Sometimes the spline is glued so well that it must be chiseled out. Care must be taken not to damage the wood on either side of the groove. After the spline is out, remove all remaining cane and glue.

Photo 2

The pressed cane to be used in the seat should be soaked in warm water for four hours to make it pliable and allowed to drip dry for a few minutes before using. In the illustrated sequence, a different open weave design was substituted for the damaged closed weave cane originally used. At this time, soak the replacement spline for about ten minutes. The spline should be a couple of inches longer than necessary (it will be trimmed in the chair). Some seats have square corners. Four pieces of spline should be cut with mitered corners. Test the fit before soaking these pieces.

Place the sheet of cane (shiny side up) on the chair seat with the weave lined up perpendicular to the front of the chair. Using a wooden wedge with a point about one-half the thickness of the groove, lightly tap several inches of the cane into the groove at the back center of the chair. Drive a temporary piece of spline about two inches long into this area. Do the same with the front center of the chair.

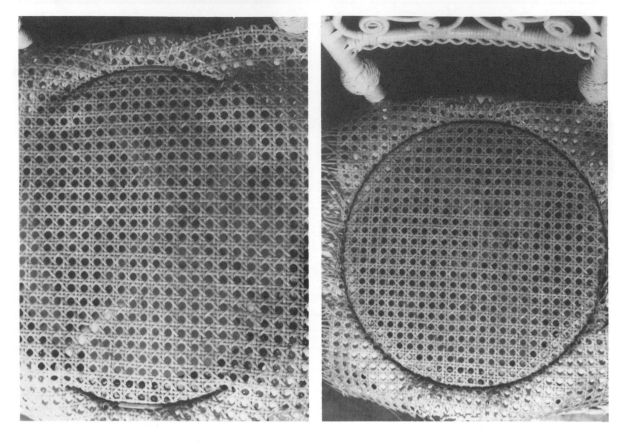

3

4

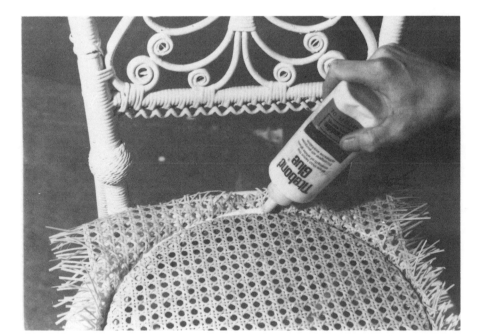

5

Photo 3

Both temporary pieces of spline are in place.

Photo 4

Tap cane into the groove the entire way around. Do not try to tap the cane to the bottom of the groove with one blow. You must stretch the cane gently. The cane is susceptible to damage at this point, so proceed slowly. Remove both pieces of temporary spline. Check to see that the cane is pressed to the bottom of the groove.

Photo 5

Squeeze a generous bead of glue into the groove. I prefer Titebond® glue.

6

7

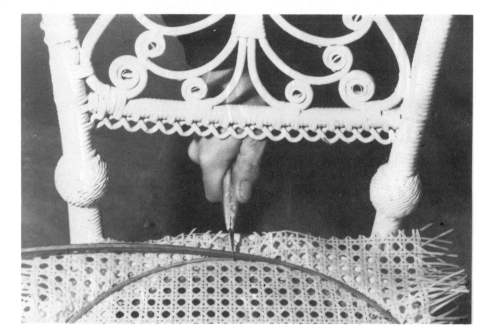

Photo 6

Using a wooden wedge with an end approximately the width of the spline, start tapping in the spline at the back center of the chair. Tap until the spline protrudes about one-eighth inch above the groove.

Photo 7

Carefully cut the spline so that the two ends meet without any gap between them.

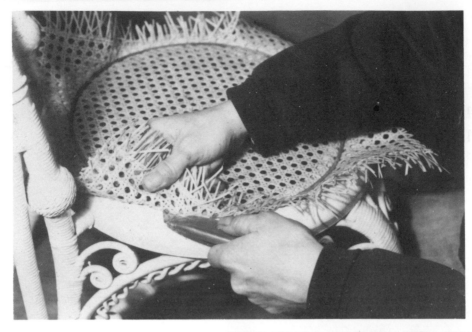

8

9

Photo 8

Wipe off the excess glue that was squeezed out when the spline was tapped into the groove. A sponge and warm water work well. Cut off the excess cane webbing around the outside of the spline. Use the wedge to tap the spline down until it is level with the seat frame. Again, wipe off any excess glue and let the glue dry twenty-four hours before using the chair.

Photo 9

Here is the finished chair seat.

V. FINISHING

Introduction to Finishing

Wicker furniture takes on many looks in today's settings. It is mellow with natural varnish, gleams in traditional white, or sports decorator colors or even two-tone finishes. This section will show you how to achieve a professional finish that suits your decorating purposes.

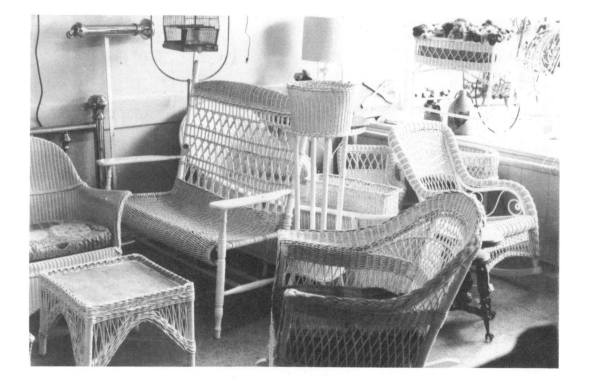

Cleaning

Some pieces of wicker need only a good cleaning to look attractive. If you have an air compressor and blow gun, go over the whole piece, taking special care to get accumulated dust and grime out of all the crevices. A vacuum cleaner with a brush attachment could also work. Next, a solution of warm, soapy water and a very soft bristle scrub brush should be used. The water should be used sparingly. Let the furniture dry completely before any painting or varnishing is done.

Sanding

Painted wicker furniture often has rough spots due to chipped or flaking paint or particles trapped in the paint film. These areas should be sanded to take away the roughness. The best method is to use a Sand-O-Flex® sander mounted on a portable drill. This type of sander does a remarkable job in a very short time. See Appendix A for further information about this product. Lacking this tool, one should sand by hand, using a folded sheet of very fine sandpaper. Badly worn areas of fiber rush should be sanded carefully to prevent tearing the surface.

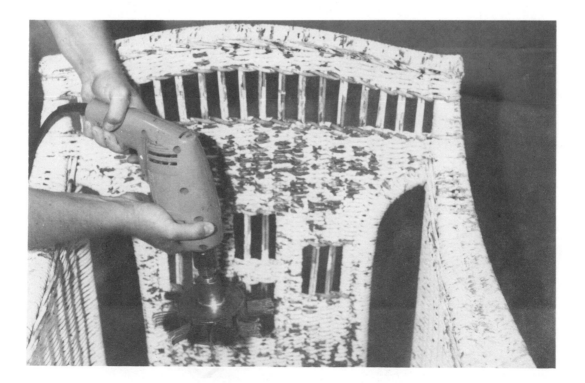

Singeing

Prior to priming, all repaired areas should be singed with a propane torch, whether repairs were made with reed or fiber rush. Also, any other roughened areas should be singed. This is done to remove the whiskerlike fibers. To paint or varnish without removing these fibers would result in a very rough surface unpleasant not only to the eye but also to the touch.

When singeing, be sure to keep the torch moving at all times and at an adequate distance from the material to avoid scorching. Practice in an inconspicuous place until you feel confident. Also, torch from all sides to completely remove all small fibers. Make several light passes over an area rather than try to accomplish the task in just one pass.

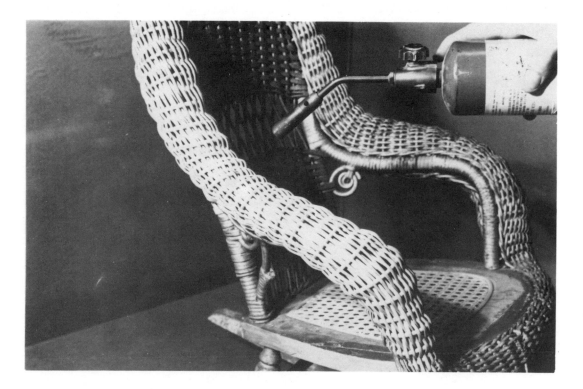

The Pros and Cons of Stripping

YOU MAY ...

* remove shellac from table tops or reed surfaces. Use a straight solution of household ammonia with a very soft brush or rag in a well ventilated area.

* remove paint or varnish from table tops with any commercial paint remover. Remove braid from table edge before stripping the top to avoid dripping remover on the braid.

I STRONGLY RECOMMEND THAT YOU DO NOT ...

* strip paint or varnish from any reed furniture, whether by hand or by commercially dipping in a tank. From the examples of stripping I have seen, there is irreparable damage done in the form of roughened areas that even singeing with a torch and sanding will not remove and a general weakening of the reed. A piece may appear to have been satisfactorily stripped, only to have defects appear after application of new paint or varnish.

UNDER NO CIRCUMSTANCES SHOULD YOU ...

* strip fiber rush furniture because the chemicals cause the paper to deteriorate and scrubbing to remove the old paint or varnish roughens the surface irreparably.

2

1

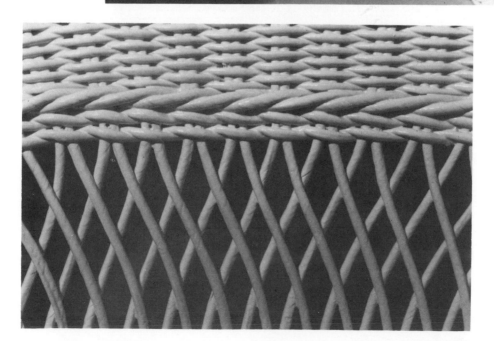

3

Photo 1

All of the light colored areas on this table are roughened from stripping.

Photo 2

The table has been primed and given a top coat—all that is necessary for most wicker in good condition. The addition of paint only serves to further emphasize the major damage caused by stripping. Moreover, when repainting a stripped piece there is a tendency to put on almost as much paint as was removed in an effort to cover all the roughened spots.

Photo 3

This is what fiber rush in good condition looks like when properly finished with primer and one coat of paint.

Touching Up Natural Wicker

Wicker furniture, whether made from reed or fiber rush, stained and finished with a coating of shellac, varnish or lacquer, is said to have a "natural" finish. Staining repaired areas to match the existing finish on this type of furniture requires patience and experimentation. Sometimes a pre-mixed color of stain (whether oil or water base) from the local hardware or paint store is just perfect. Other times, several cans of stain with the same base (water or oil) may be mixed to achieve the proper color. Experiment in an inconspicuous place and go from light to dark. A stained area can always be made darker but not lighter. For staining these repair areas I have found artists' acrylic paints to be the best medium for achieving the exact color. A selection of yellow ochre, burnt sienna, raw sienna, burnt umber, Indian red, black, and white will handle practically any staining situation. Moreover, artists' acrylic paint is the only medium which will successfully stain cane wrapping. In this case, the acrylic paint is put on more as a paint and makes an opaque stain.

In some cases, a piece of old wicker has a mottled effect with the outer surfaces of the weavers light in color from being rubbed and worn over the years, while the interstices are still very dark. When trying to stain repaired areas on a piece like this, I judiciously scorch the area with the propane torch before using the acrylic paint. Also, I use sandpaper to rub off some of the stain to simulate years of wear.

Acrylic paint can also be used to color the heads of replacement brads so they blend in with the piece. When replacing only a spoke or two in a stained piece of reed furniture, it is best to stain the replacement parts before inserting them into the piece. If the replacement parts need to be soaked for bending, use acrylic paint after soaking. Sand any fuzz off before staining.

Whether touching up small areas or recoating an entire piece of natural wicker, I recommend using varnish with a soya or linseed oil base. The new plastic or polyurethane varnishes are to be avoided as they do not adhere well to the original finish. Varnishes may be obtained in different sheens. A high gloss varnish produces the hardest coating. Use the same varnish as the primer and the top coat.

Touching Up Painted Wicker

If after cleaning your wicker the finish is still unattractive, it may only require touching up nicked spots. Touching up painted wicker is, of course, easiest to do if you have some leftover paint of the proper color. If the nick is a bad one (exposing raw fiber rush or reed), it should be sealed first with 3 Purpose B-I-N Primer Sealer. This is discussed in detail on the following page. In cases where you desire to touch up nicks on wicker for which you do not have the proper color, use artists' acrylic paint which is available in small tubes from an art supply store. This paint is superb for touch ups because it dries quickly and can be painted over latex or oil base paints. Acrylic paints also are useful to fill and camouflage tack holes. If you are unable to get the correct color at first, merely change your mixture and paint over what you have put on. It is not within the scope of this book to teach color mixing. If you are not sure what you need to mix a particular color, take a paint chip from your wicker to the paint store for guidance.

Application of Paint and Varnish

Wicker furniture is best primed, painted, and varnished by spraying. Not only does brushing require great care and time, but it tends to wipe the outer surfaces too thin for durability while it piles up the finishing materials in the spaces between the weave. On the other hand, spray application lays on an adequate coat on the outer surfaces and a minimum amount within the weave where it is least needed.

For the most professional looking job an air compressor and spray gun are needed. You may be able to rent a spray unit in your area. Spray cans of B-I-N and of enamels are also available, but are best for touch ups rather than for entire pieces.

All primers, paints, and varnishes should be put on in thin coats. Thin coats dry faster, are more durable, and look better than heavy applications. Paints and varnishes should be strained before using.

Priming for Painting

The key factor in obtaining a professional looking paint job with a durable finish and an even sheen is the use of a good primer. A primer seals the surface and provides a good base for adhesion of the top coat of paint. I tried many paint products for priming with little success until I discovered 3 Purpose B-I-N Primer Sealer. B-I-N is a mixture of white shellac and white pigment and dries to a flat white which is dry to handle in fifteen to twenty minutes and ready for a final finish in forty-five minutes. This product does a superb job of sealing and dries to a very tough, durable surface. Its unusual adhesion makes it perfect for hard-to-grip surfaces such as wicker. It seals so effectively that one coat will usually cover even a black piece that is to be painted a light color and it can be used under any finish coat of gloss, semi-gloss, or flat paint whether oil-base or water emulsion (latex). (See Appendix A, p. 159 for manufacturer.)

B-I-N is also an excellent primer for new table tops and all replacement reed or fiber rush. On these "raw" surfaces, it is sometimes necessary to use more than one coat, owing to their extreme porosity.

After the prime coat of B-I-N is dry, lightly sand any rough spots. All table tops should be lightly sanded before going on to the top or finish coat. Dust the piece thoroughly before proceeding to the top coat.

Top Coat of Paint

Once you have decided upon the color and sheen, choose any good enamel or latex paint. The paint should also be chosen according to where the furniture is to be used. Enamel is the most commonly used paint on wicker and the one I prefer. Cheap paints are no bargain. Buy only the best.

On a piece properly primed with B-I-N Primer Sealer, I recommend only one thin top coat of paint. This provides all the protection that is needed, reduces the likelihood of runs and sags, avoids filling the interstices with thick accumulations of paint, and lessens the possibility of chipping.

Two-Tone Effects

In the past many pieces of wicker had the braid and other accents painted in a contrasting color to the rest of the piece.

Another type of two-tone effect used on wicker is achieved by painting the whole piece one color and, when dry, putting on an overtone of another color which is immediately wiped with rags until the desired effect is accomplished. Many color combinations were used in the past, ranging from forest green over bright orange to light brown over ivory.

Caring for the Finish

Keep fiber rush out of the weather.

Cover wicker furniture when not in use (in a summer home, for instance).

Vacuum with a soft brush.

Clean periodically with a damp cloth to remove dirt.

Keep a small container of paint handy for occasional touch ups.

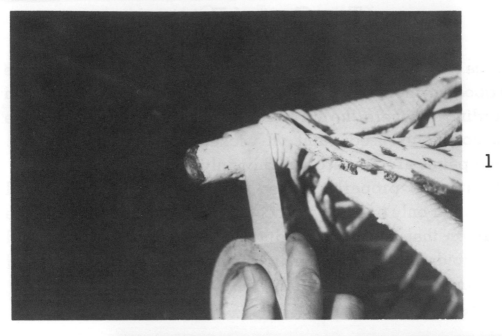

1

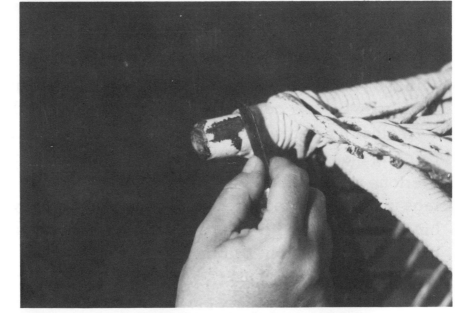

2

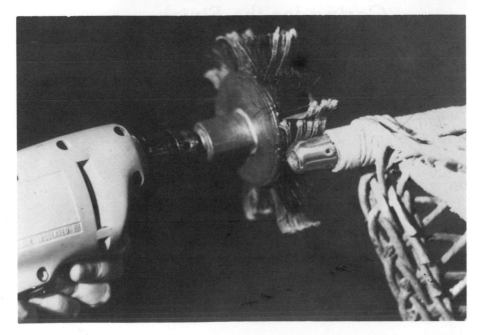

3

Polishing Leg Caps

Metal caps were often used on wicker furniture to cover the ends of legs. When these caps were intended to be painted, they were made from steel; when intended to be decorative, they were either steel with brass plating or solid brass. Polished brass leg caps are attractive on natural as well as on painted wicker.

Over the years the brass plated or solid brass leg caps darken and lose their vitality or, as on much painted wicker, are painted over. If you like the look of polished brass, check the leg caps on your furniture by lightly scraping a small area. If they prove to be brass, follow the directions below for polishing. A small, easily accomplished detail of restoration such as this makes an amazing amount of difference in the final appearance of a piece.

Photo 1

If the finish on the leg is good, wrap with masking tape for protection while polishing.

Photo 2

Lightly scrape off old paint or varnish with a pocket knife.

Photo 3

Use the Sand-O-Flex® with a medium grit abrasive for polishing the leg cap. If the cap is brass plated, take care not to sand through the plating. The Sand-O-Flex® polishes the cap quickly to a gleaming finish.

APPENDICES

A. Suppliers

Repair Materials

(These companies carry a large selection of reed, cane, and fiber rush, and other weaving materials and tools. If you are uncertain what weaving materials are needed to make a repair, send them a sample. They will match the material and send the correct one to you.)

H. H. Perkins
10 South Bradley Road
Woodbridge, CT 06525

Cane and Basket Supply Co.
1283 S. Cochran Avenue
Los Angeles, CA 90019

Connecticut Cane and Reed Co.
P.O. Box 1276
Manchester, CT 06040

The Wicker Shop
2190 Marshall Avenue
St. Paul, MN 55104

The Brass Tree
308 N. Main
St. Charles, MO 63301

New Hampshire Cane and Reed
65 Turnpike St. Box 176
Suncook, NH 03275

The Caning Shop
926 Gilman St.
Berkeley, CA 94710

Frank's Cane and Rush Supply
7244 Heil Avenue
Huntington Beach, CA 92647

WSI Distributors
P.O. Box 1235
St. Charles, MO 63302
   (Wholesale Only)

Tools

Merit Abrasive Products, Inc.
201 W. Manville St.
Compton, CA 90224
   (manufacturer and supplier
   of Sand-O-Flex®)

Senco Fastening Systems
8485 Broadwell Road
Cincinnati, Ohio 45244
   (air staplers, nailers and
   tackers)

Petersen Manufacturing
   Company, Inc.
De Witt, Nebraska 68341
   (manufacturers of
   VISE-GRIP® tools)

Finishing Materials and Glues

William Zinsser and Company
39 Belmont Drive
Somerset, NJ 08873
   (makers of 3 Purpose B-I-N,
   a superior primer-sealer)

Franklin Chemical
   Industries, Inc.
2020 Bruck St.
P.O. Box 07802
Columbus, Ohio 43207
   (makers of Titebond®
   and Home and Craft®
   glues)

B. General Working Tips

It's not uncommon to find a seat where the cane is unbroken but the seat sags. The sag can often be removed by wetting the underside of the cane and letting the seat dry. Sometimes this process needs to be repeated several times to achieve the desired result.

Elevate the work to a comfortable height and make sure you have good lighting.

If your length of pre-soaked reed seems to lose suppleness before the repair is completed, wet with a sponge.

A Phillips screwdriver is often helpful to enlarge holes to pass reed through.

Put boards under the runners to steady a rocking chair while making repairs.

Often to blend a repair in fiber rush it is necessary to hammer the repaired area lightly to flatten it so it will match the surrounding material. Also, twist fiber rush tighter or untwist as necessary to blend in with old material.

GLOSSARY

Braid
>decorative strip formed by weaving strands together.

Fiber rush
>manmade fiber produced by twisting paper.

Hand caning
>the process of passing strands of cane across a chair seat or back and then through holes drilled around the edge of the framework to form a decorative pattern.

Leg
>the upright support structure below the seat level.

Leg cap
>a small, metal cap often found on the end of a leg of wicker furniture, its purpose being both decorative and functional for protection of both the wicker wrapping and the flooring.

Loom woven
>wicker furniture made from sheets of machine woven fiber rush fitted over a framework.

Mortise
>a cavity in a piece of wood prepared to receive a similarly shaped projection or tenon of another piece.

Open work
>areas without weavers where only the spokes show.

Post
>the upright support structure above the seat level.

Pressed cane
>cane woven into sheets by machine and held into a routed groove with spline.

Priming
>use of a first coat to seal the surface and provide a good base for adhesion of the top coat of finish.

Reed
>cut from rattan palm and available in various shapes such as round, flat, and half round.

Runners
>the curved pieces of wood upon which a rocking chair rests.

Serpentine parts
>hollow, curved areas most commonly seen as chair arms and backs.

Scrollwork
>decorative work ranging from simple, broad loops to complex curlicues. More common on earlier reed pieces.

Singeing
>use of a propane torch to remove whisker-like fibers from reed or fiber rush prior to finishing.

Spline
>triangular reed that holds pressed cane into a routed groove.

Spokes
>the strands that form the basis upon which the weaving is done.

Tenon
>a projection on the end of a piece of wood shaped for insertion into a mortise.

Top coat
>the final layer of paint or varnish that is applied over the prime coat.

Weavers
>the strands used to weave over and under the spokes.

BIBLIOGRAPHY

Corbin, Patricia. All About Wicker. New York: E.P. Dutton, 1978.

Miller, Bruce W. and Widess, Jim. The Caner's Handbook. New York: Van Nostrand Reinhold Company, 1983.

Saunders, Richard. Collecting and Restoring Wicker Furniture. New York: Crown Publishers, Inc., 1976.

Shirley, Glyndon E.. Great Grandmother's Wicker Furniture 1880's-1920's. Burlington, Iowa: Craftsman Press, 1978.

Weiss, Jeffrey. Cornerstone Collector's Guide to Wicker. New York: Simon and Schuster, 1981.

INDEX

braid
   how to make, 52
   piecing, 49-51
   reasons for making, 52
   removal from table tops, 118-119
   replacing a section of, 53
   replacing entire length of, 54-57

cane
   manufacture of, 2
   notes on, 137
   sagging seat of, 160
   seat replacement, 138-145
   using, 22

cleaning, 147

fiber rush
   blending in repairs of, 160
   caring for finish of, 155
   distinguishing from reed, 9
   evaluating condition of, 11
   history of, 2
   sanding, 147
   singeing, 148
   stripping, 149-151
   touching up natural, 152
   touching up painted, 153
   using, 22
   wire core, 11, 39
   wrapping with, 46

finishing
   application of paint and varnish, 153
   caring for the finish, 155
   cleaning, 147
   evaluating an existing finish, 12-13
   introduction to, 146
   polishing leg caps, 156-157
   priming for painting, 154
   sanding, 147
   singeing, 148
   stripping, 149-151
   table tops, 123
   top coat of paint, 155
   touching up natural wicker, 152
   touching up painted wicker, 153
   two-tone effects, 155

floor lamp
    leaning, 132-135
    woven base repair, 136

framework
    broken dowel under seat, 64-67
    evaluating condition of, 9
    notes on, 58
    plywood foundation, 74-81
    repairing a broken post or leg, 68-73
    repairing loose runner on rocking chair, 82-85
    replacing broken tenon on rocking chair, 86-87
    replacing runners on rocking chair, 88-93
    replacing seat support slats, 67
    tightening existing braces, 59
    tightening joints on frame by replacing loose nails with screws, 60-61
    use of chair braces, 62-63

glue, use of on woven material, 22

leg, repairing a broken, 68-73

leg caps, polishing, 156-157

Lloyd, Marshall, 2

loom woven, 2

materials, list of, 18, 19

post, repairing a broken, 68-73

reed
    check for suppleness, 11
    history of, 2
    if loses suppleness, 160
    reducing diameter of, 20-21
    substituting for fiber rush, 38-41
    touching up natural, 152
    touching up painted, 153
    types of, 18, 19
    using, 22

repairs
    broken dowel under seat, 64-67
    caning, notes on, 137
    frame repair using chair braces, 62-63
    leaning floor lamp, 132-135
    making braid, 52-53
    making scrollwork, 98-101
    mending a hole, 30-31

repairs, continued
  notes on frame, 58
  piecing braid, 48-51
  piecing spokes on serpentine arm, 108-109
  piecing weavers on serpentine arm, 104-107
  plywood foundation, 74-81
  pressed cane seat replacement, 138-145
  reattaching scrollwork, 94-95
  repair of a woven lamp base, 136
  repairing a broken post or leg, 68-73
  repairing broken tenon on rocking chair, 86-87
  repairing broken weavers by piecing, 24-27
  repairing loose runner on rocking chair, 82-85
  replacing a section of braid, 53
  replacing a table top, 118-123
  replacing entire length of braid, 54-57
  replacing pairing weave, 28-29
  replacing runners on rocking chair, 88-93
  replacing scrollwork, 96-97
  replacing seat support slats, 67
  replacing serpentine arm 110-117
  replacing spokes in entirety, 42-43
  serpentine arm, notes on, 102-103
  skirt replacement, 124-131
  spoke continues as part of braid, 36-37
  spoke replacement, 32-35
  substituting reed for fiber rush, 38-41
  tightening existing braces, 59
  tightening joints on frame by replacing loose nails with screws, 60-61
  wooden wedges aid in wrapping, 47
  wrapping with cane, 44-45
  wrapping with fiber rush, 46

sanding, 147

scrollwork
  making, 98-101
  reattaching, 94-95
  replacing, 96-97

serpentine parts
  notes on repair of, 102-103
  piecing spokes on, 108-109
  piecing weavers on, 104-107
  replacing, 110-117

singeing, 148

skirt replacement, 124-131

spoke
  continues as part of braid, 36-37
  determining condition of, 11
  piecing on serpentine arm, 108-109
  replacement of, 32-35
  replacing in entirety, 42-43
  substituting reed for fiber rush, 38-41
  with wire core, 11, 39

stripping, 13, 149-151

table tops, replacement of, 118-123

tools, 18-19, 160

weaver
  evaluating condition of, 10-11
  mending a hole, 30-31
  piecing on serpentine arm, 104-107
  repairing by piecing, 24-27
  repairing pairing weave, 28-29

wicker
  definition of, 2
  uses of, 3

wrapping
  cane, 44-45
  fiber rush, 46
  wooden wedges aid in, 47

Additional copies of this book may be obtained by writing to:

Duncan-Holmes Publishing Company
P.O. Box 481
Syracuse, Indiana 46567

An order form and additional information will be promptly forwarded for your convenience.